IDENTITY-CRISIS
CAUSE AND CURE

*Who determines
my identity,
my dignity,
my destiny?*

by
RON CRAIG

**Author and Pastor of
Living Way Fellowship**

Identity-Crisis — Cause and Cure
Copyright © 2024 by Ron Craig

ISBN: 979-8895312025 (sc)
ISBN: 979-8895312032 (e)

All rights reserved. No part of this publication may be reproduced, distributed, or transmitted in any form or by any means, including photocopying, recording, or other electronic or mechanical methods, without the prior written permission of the publisher, except in the case brief quotations embodied in critical reviews and other noncommercial uses permitted by copyright law.

The views expressed in this book are solely those of the author and do not necessarily reflect the views of the publisher, and the publisher hereby disclaims any responsibility for them.

Writers' Branding
(877) 608-6550
www.writersbranding.com
media@writersbranding.com

Technical page

Unless otherwise noted, all Scripture references are from the King James Version—with some rewording for clarity. Within Scripture quotations, all words in *italics* and/or *ALL CAPITALS* are for emphasis by this author. And, some of this author's own comments are in *italics* or *ALL CAPITALS* for emphasis on some Bible-Truths.

Contents

Introduction ix
Chapter 1 — Adam's standing with God 1
Chapter 2 — Adam's pre-sin-lifestyle 5
Chapter 3 — Restoration of the blessings 15
Chapter 4 — Adam united with Satan 21
Chapter 5 — Satan's-evil-designs 31
Chapter 6 — Satan's-subtle-strategies 41
Chapter 7 — The biblical-case—Acts 17:26 51
Chapter 8 — Historical-evidence of the fall 59
Chapter 9 — Human-hopelessness 67
Chapter 10 — Hefty-price-tag—Hebrews 2:14 77
Chapter 11 — Total-redemption-package 87
Chapter 12 — No longer identified with Adam 99
Chapter 13 — Death to our old-nature 107
Chapter 14 — Our brand-new-life-in-Christ 115
Chapter 15 — All things are ours in Christ! 123
Chapter 16 — Improper-view of the how-to 133
Chapter 17 — Legal and vital-sides of redemption 145
Chapter 18 — God's eternal-seed-principle 155
Identity-crisis cause and cure in a nutshell 165

Acknowledgements

I acknowledge first of all, Jesus Christ my Lord; and the One Who has given me the revelations contained in this book. I also thank my wife Joan, and all the other members of Living Way Fellowship, for their sustained patience and moral support of me in all my authoring endeavors. May this work honor all of you!

Introduction

Our Lord does not unveil to anyone His life-changing biblical-realities for the benefit of that one person alone. Bible-Truth targets everyone within the Body of Christ! Indeed, every person on earth is an intended-recipient. Nevertheless, *the Lord's church must FIRST understand those biblical-realities before the world has opportunity to hear about that redemption which is available only to people who trust in Jesus Christ for their salvation.* For, the lost normally do not search for God; at least where He may be found. (Romans 10:20) *This lost-world is in desperate need of SALVATION-TRUTH; which resides in Holy Scripture—or ministered by those who are familiar enough with Bible-Truth to believe it, live by it, and fill other people in on it.* Tragically today, MANY Christians suffer from just about as great a *LACK* of knowledge of Gospel-Truth as does the *LOST*-world! *The multitude of discrepancies between the TEACHINGS of the branches of the splintered-church magnifies the stark-reality that they all cannot be correct in every doctrine and practice they all cling to with religious-fervency!* See Hosea 4:6.

For *MOST* of my life, our Savior has been educating me in *Scripture-University. Early on I garnered only bits and pieces of some eternal-realities—which I now know to be of supreme-importance to the spiritual-pulse of the Redeemer's church. Those bits and pieces fit together to frame the whole-counsel-of-God-theology—revealing the LIFESTYLE God desires for every Christian.* (Acts 2:40, 5:20, 20:20, 27, 24:14, Hebrews 10:20) Moreover,...

The more I study God's Word, the more the message of this book is confirmed within me. My in-depth-study of the believer's *IDENTIFICATION* with Christ has done more to open my eyes to Bible-Truth about God's plan for mankind than I have found in any book I have read outside the Bible. *And, all the conclusions presented in this book are based upon and backed by an abundance of Scripture passages. Thus, I URGE the readers to read ALL references.* A good starting place is Acts 17:11-12: *You will then understand my purpose for this volume!*

I have utilized a number of sound-Bible-principles in this book to make SURE what I have written is accurate and beneficial to the readers. The principles themselves have been derived from the Scriptures; and totally agree with the overall-Scripture-picture. For, *I carry out all my arguments to their logical-biblical-conclusions; providing two or more Scriptures which are in agreement with one another pertaining to the subject at hand; and which do not conflict with any other clear-biblical-statement. That is the principle of biblical-consistency.* Moreover, *I focus on who is doing the communicating in the passage, and the person or persons being communicated unto—which ensures an ACCURATE-PRESENTATION of the Gospel.*

This unique-volume will HELP readers discover their God-ordained-PURPOSE for inhabiting this planet—and will help them cooperate with God to fulfill that purpose: Showing how to shed the satanic-shackles of religious-tradition; and be in a good position to HELP loved ones, neighbors, and perhaps even a few enemies; as well as glorify the Savior in the process. So, to begin!

NEVER before in the church's history has there been such a combination of Bible-Truth-preaching, along with religious-tradition; or God's Inspired-Word mingled with demonic-doctrines! (1 Timothy 4:1-2) On any Sunday, in most any city of the civilized-countries on earth, you can enter a building of one particular style of church-architecture, hear a little Scripture-reading *spiced with a large-portion of human-error,* depart that building, go down the street a few blocks, and enter another edifice boasting a completely different architectural-style, and partake of *a whole-different-menu of men's-ideas about life,* and perhaps, a few crumbs from God's Holy Word. Although such conditions do not curse *EVERY* church-setting, *THE PERCENTAGE of such occurrences is much too high.* The *HEAD* of the church cannot be *PLEASED* with such hypocrisy prevailing in His church—and the Body of Christ certainly cannot afford to continue that downward-spiral! Get a glimpse of Christ's response to such conditions in Revelation chapters-two and three.

It seems to matter not to many of today's-religious-leaders that there exist so many differences among the different-segments of that entity known as the Body of Christ. Keeping pet-denominational-programs intact is *MORE* important to those denominational-leaders than building the Kingdom of God; *AND* maintaining a God-honoring-Christian-witness before the lost-world!

Is it any wonder that so many people who *CLAIM* to be Christians are *CONFUSED?* And should it be such a surprise to ecclesiastical-leaders that the world laughs at the splintered-church—and that *MOST* churches are of *LITTLE-THREAT* to the devil's dark-kingdom?

Where does Jesus fit into this pitiful-scenario? How many of our religious-activities would Jesus dare to be involved in? Maybe 50%; perhaps, no more than 10%? The Evangelist Billy Graham said that 95% of church-activities would continue, even without the Holy Spirit! And he reported that sad-statistic many decades ago.

Is it not possible for God's people to do things God's way? *That is possible, IF WE ARE WILLING to do things His way!* What is the secret of discovering God's ways, AND WALKING IN THEM? This wise-answer: *"When all else fails read THE INSTRUCTIONS!" Bible-instructions, that is!* The primary-purpose of this volume is to point people to God's-Written-Instructions—the Holy Bible.

YET, Scripture itself is a mystery to many believers. *Most professing-Christians assume that only seminary-graduates are qualified to comprehend God's Word.* But Seminary-graduates understand the Bible-message no more than anyone else! You read correctly. Only people who are spiritually-open to spiritual-realities are in the spiritual-position to understand spiritual-realities; and that is offered to everybody living on earth—not only to seminarians. *Ecclesiastical-education does not produce openness to spiritual-truth. Because, that RARE-quality originates within the spirit of a believer—springing from a real-life-encounter with the Savior—and is possessed by people INSIDE and OUTSIDE the classroom. For,...*

"We have received not the spirit of the world, but the Spirit which is of God; that we might [spiritually-]*know* [all of] *the things that are freely given to us by God."* (1 Corinthians 2:12) And verse-thirteen: *"These things we speak, NOT in words that man's* [worldly, or seminary-] *wisdom teaches; BUT, the things the Holy Ghost* [Spirit] *teaches—comparing spiritual-things with spiritual."* For, "It is written: *'Eye has not seen nor ear heard* [meaning spiritual-truths cannot be PERCEIVED by the natural-senses], *neither have entered into the hearts of men the things which God has prepared for those who love Him. BUT, God has revealed them to us by His Spirit: For the Spirit searches all things; even the deep-things of God.'"* Divine-things cannot be understood by man's intellect: *"The things of God knows no man; but the Spirit of God* [knows all about them]." (1 Corinthians 2:9-11)

God having inspired men to *PEN* the Bible, we must get acquainted with Him Who inspired them *TO PEN IT* before we *CAN GRASP* what they *PENNED!* Who would know that communication better than God Himself? No one can bypass the Divine-system of revelation! Check out Proverbs 2:7, 4:7, 9:10 and 30:5-6. Moreover,...

Before we can *successfully-practice* New-Testament-Christianity, *we must understand what it means to be a Christian.* There is just as much confusion regarding that area of biblical-reality today as there is any other! *Whereas many insist that we must be baptized with the PROPER-formula to be saved, others teach that seekers must unite with the PROPER-branch of the church.* I too searched for that *just-right-denomination* for years. *My eyes were finally opened to Bible-Truth that redemption comes not from ANY denomination; nor is it received by baptismal-formulas.* True-salvation is experienced only in Jesus Christ—and that only by faith and obedience!

I do not have a personal-patent on discerning Bible-Truth: But in this book, I am presenting to the readers *powerful-spiritual-tools,* by which those who truly want to learn the Bible-Truth—what redemption is really all about—can learn all they need to know about it. *Those tools can also be used in the defense against the devil's every-attack on our every-Christian-endeavor.*

Now some KEY-principles of biblical-comprehension: And *KEY* is the appropriate-term to use. There is some key that unlocks every letter and/or book of the Bible: Sometimes it is a verse; sometimes only one word. One example is John's first letter. *Some insist the word love is the key that opens that little epistle; and love truly is a recurring-theme in it. But the key-word in John's first epistle is KNOW. I have to get to KNOW God before I can*

LOVE HIM. John taught that my *KNOWING* God's love toward me is what enables me to *BELIEVE* in His love toward me—and *RECIPROCATE* in like-kind—love Him back. (1 John 4:7-9, 16, 19) By coming to *KNOW* God's love for me, I *KNOW* I have passed from death into life; and that I love *OTHERS* who are in Christ. (1 John 2:5, 3:14, 5:1-2) *The Divine-order—KNOWING comes before LOVING.* Also see John 17:3 and 1 John 4:20-21.

The book of Hebrews is another example. The word that *UNLOCKS* that letter is *BETTER*. Hebrews tells us the *NEW COVENANT* has *BETTER* sacrifices, promises, assurances and Mediator than did that Old Covenant. That one *KEY*-word gives us a *BETTER* understanding of what the book of Hebrews is all about.

The key-verse that unlocks the message of the Bible itself is Deuteronomy 29:29: "The secret things belong to the Lord our God: But the things which are revealed belong to us and our children forever—that we may do [practice] *ALL* the words of this law." God has to reveal something before we can *KNOW* about it. And, what He has revealed to us, He expects us to heed and obey!

The *KEY*-word in this book is *IDENTIFICATION*. And even though the word itself is not found, at least in the King James Bible, *the identification-principle is in every Bible-book. IDENTIFICATION IS KEY TO understanding human-nature, how this world became sinful in the first place, and what powers determine our destiny.*

The biggest-crisis on the planet today is the identity-crisis. Multitudes of people know not who they are! The Bible identifies different-identities; *AND tells us how to change our current-identity, if we do not like it: For OUR TEMPORAL-identity determines OUR ETERNAL-destiny!* And most people are unaware of even that Bible-Truth.

Chapter One

Adam's standing with God

A most-enlightening Bible-Truth is Adam's *LEGAL-STANDING* with his Creator. What does that mean and what does it have to do with you and me? Everything! Adam has determined our condition. He being the first human being, *Adam's relationship with God would also determine the relationship of other human beings with God—BOTH before and after his sin*. Therefore, if Adam fared well in the beginning, *AND* maintained that right-standing with God, *his offspring would also be blessed forever*. However, if for some reason Adam *forfeited* his original-relationship with God and started reproducing after his *NEW*-kind, *Adam's offspring would be polluted just like Adam!* The Bible-principle of *like-parent-like-offspring* is of primary-importance to *ALL* living-things. According to Genesis-chapter-one, *GOD MADE EVERY LIVING-THING TO REPRODUCE AFTER ITS OWN KIND*. Luke 3:38 says Adam was a son of God; made in God's image. *AND*, Genesis 5:3 says that Seth was in Adam's image; *made like Adam's-kind. When Adam sinned, his nature was altered—he afterward reproducing offspring with the same altered-nature—a sinner by nature—and so with every generation since!* Even in light of that,...

One extreme-view of *MAN* portrays Adam as a *GOD*; whereas the opposite end of that *speculation-spectrum* sees little difference in Adam's make-up before or after his fall. Some preachers *IMPLY* that the original-Adam *WAS DISPOSED TO SIN* through a moral-flaw lodged in his *PRIMAL-NATURE*. *Such a religious-concept of Adam stems from a demonic-teaching on the total-depravity of humankind—invented by the devil, and pushed on the church by John Calvin, and his deceived-followers.* The proponents of that demonic-doctrine contend that even being born again does not eradicate that sinful-nature. The contention that even the sacrificial-work of Christ on that cross came short of abolishing our sin-nature, and fully reconciling us back to God, is one step away from asserting that Adam had some moral-flaw abiding within him, even before he committed sin. John Calvin actually taught that falsehood! Such a fatalistic-view of people paints a fatalistic-picture of God! For, if Adam's original-nature had a negative-bent, then God Himself was guilty of Adam's sin! *Such a claim is nothing more than a humanistic-excuse for people to continue living in sin.* See Romans 5:17-21, 6:1-2, 6. Bible-Truth is,...

Adam was not some kind of god; elevating mankind to a higher position than God made him to be. Adam's Creator did not announce: "Let us create another god." But said: "Let us make man." (Genesis 1:26) However, Adam was created in the *IMAGE* of God; which means that *God made man as much like Himself as He could possibly fashion a created-being!* Now think about this: *That God has always been God constitutes Him as God.* How could God Who has always been God create some other being as God, even though that other being has not always existed? God was God from all eternity!

Although God strictly-prohibited adding to His Word one's PERSONAL-OPINIONS of His Word (Deuteronomy 4:2, Proverbs 30:6, Revelation 22:18-19), certain Bible-teachers contend that John 10:34-36, quoting Psalms 82:6, declares that Adam was *a god* over this planet, *in the same sense that his Creator was God over all of the heavens.* However, *Christ quoted that Psalm merely to prove that, in LIGHT of that Old Testament passage, His claim to be God's Son was only reasonable.* The eighty-second-Psalm *laments that some who were in positions of judgeship in Israel had abused their political-position to oppress their own countrymen.* The psalmist did not suggest that God had created Adam *AS* a god. In fact, *the psalm is filled with negative-connotations regarding those rulers, and did not reveal God's original or future-plan for man.* Adam was never god over the planet; but under God was the caretaker of it! (Genesis 2:15)

Jeremiah 10:11 says: "The gods that have not made the heavens, and this earth; even they [manmade-idols and demons behind those idols] *WILL PERISH* from the earth and from under these heavens." Therefore, if God *DID* intend for Adam to be a god, He changed His mind sometime later. And, 1 Corinthians 8:5-6: "(As there be many gods and many lords): But to Christians, there is but one God, the Father." Man has never been a god!

Nor does God's Word anywhere even hint that Adam was cursed with some kind of moral-flaw somewhere in his tripartite-being when God created him. Adam flawed himself by his sin against God in the Garden of Eden!

In the next chapter, I emphasize the atmosphere of that sinless-world Adam and Eve inhabited before they sinned and were separated from God. Christians today need to know about Adam's original-standing with his Creator, before sin made its debut on this planet. After this Bible-course, you will *SEE* redemption in a totally-different and greatly-improved *LIGHT*. But now this,...

Two prime-reasons it is difficult for most believers to relate to Adam's righteous-standing with his Creator on THE OTHER SIDE OF SIN—One: *They do not experience such in their entire-lifetime; although the Bible promises some of those blessings are for today. TWO: Since about*

99% of the Bible-account deals with experiences on this side of the fall, there is not a mountain of material from which to gain information on Adam's blessed-life before sin shattered his life. There is MORE of that information in the Bible than most people realize, however. So,...

HAD earth's-first-human-couple REMAINED in their original-state-of-innocence, none of humanity's current-problems would even exist, let alone prevail, in modern-society. As history unfolded, however, Eve believed the Serpent's-plan would provide them with more blessings than the Creator had—and Adam went along. The devil lured them on a destruction-path: And they FELL for it!

Adam was made the highest-class of spiritual-being, so he could enjoy an intimate-fellowship with God; and manage the rest of creation for God. Adam being able to relate to BOTH the spirit and material-realms, he would be the natural-go-between for God and this planet! But, that unique-privilege-and-position was curtailed when Adam sinned. Man became slave instead of master.

So far we have barely-introduced the revolutionary-Bible-Truth about *identification*; and have only slightly touched on the truth that *Adam and Eve lived a truly-glorious-lifestyle during their pre-transgression-days in the Garden—due to their sin-free-relationship with their Creator.* The next chapter points out some of the many benefits that first couple experienced while dwelling in a *SIN*-free, *CURSE*-free-environment. That *eye-opening, mind-reprogramming, heart-thrilling REVELATION is the very foundation, on which the remainder of this book is built!* And I believe you will be extremely-edified by that heavenly-communication. So let us begin!

Chapter Two

Adam's pre-sin-lifestyle

Luke labeled Adam the *son of God*. (Luke 3:38) *And even though the Greek huios* (son) *is not in the original-text in that verse, Luke used the same wording there as in the other verses in that genealogy of Jesus Christ.* In Luke 3:23, *the Greek word for son* (huios) *does appear, but following verses repeat the rest of that phrase over and over without including the Greek word for SON.*

People steeped in religion have little-comprehension of Adam's legal-standing with the Creator. *If somebody were to emphasize that fact, they would likely respond: "How could Adam's relationship with the Creator before he fell affect modern-society?"* The Bible-answer to that religious-question is more important than many people think. First, *it tells us Adam had a favorable-beginning. Man has not always been SUBJECT to death's dictates; as in* 1 Corinthians 15:22. *Adam's PRE-sin-experiences were vastly-different than are most human-experiences today.* WHEN did Adam's-world deteriorate? The Bible-answer to that question comes later. But now,...

Let us look at Adam's *pristine-world* and learn what it was like BEFORE HE HOOKED UP WITH THE DEVIL. *Man's original-ancestors were not rebels from the start!* At one time (Who knows for how long?), *Adam and Eve enjoyed an intimate-daily-fellowship with their Creator.* Although that activity is recorded in the chapter telling of their fall, it is at least implied there that communion with God was a daily-routine. For, Genesis 3:8 tells us: "They heard *THE VOICE* of the Lord God walking in the

GARDEN in the cool of the day." That speaks volumes about the positive-living-conditions in Adam's sinless-world. How many people in modern-society take walks with God in the cool of the day? *MOST* are too busy to *GIVE* their Creator even a passing-thought—and *MANY* who do *THINK* about God hold some weird and fearful-views about the Creator. But, *Adam and Eve expressed no dread of God BEFORE the fall.* (Genesis 2:25, 3:10) *Prior to that, they enjoyed fellowship with the Creator of the vast universe!* FANATICS today will pull all kinds of stunts to gain the attention of a sports, or movie-star; AND an autograph, of course—*and that from somebody who might possibly go to Hell when they die! Adam and Eve rubbed shoulders with Him Who brought ALL things into being; including those celebrities.* God is a genuine-Celebrity! However, instead of us trying to obtain God's autograph, He wants our names in the Lamb's Book of Life. (Luke 10:20, Revelation 3:5, 13:8, 22:19)

What *QUALIFIED* Adam and Eve to enjoy fellowship with the Creator of this universe? *They were composed of earth AND God Himself!* Genesis 2:7: *"The Lord God formed man from the DUST of the ground, and breathed into his nostrils the breath* [Spirit] *of life; and then man became a living soul."* Adam's body consisted of earth, but his life came from the breath of God. (*God does not breath oxygen! He filled Adam's dust-body with Spirit.*) The apostle Paul penned in 2 Timothy 3:16 that: *"ALL Scripture is given by INSPIRATION OF GOD."* The Greek word rendered INSPIRATION there literally means God-breathed—which is how the Creator *ANIMATED* Adam. God actually deposited into Adam part of Himself (His Spirit-Breath), which automatically qualified Adam to engage in an intimate-fellowship with his very Creator. And, because Eve had been constructed out of Adam's body, with God's Spirit-life in it, *she had the same right* to fellowship with God as Adam had—because both her spiritual and bodily-composition sprang from Adam. See Genesis 2:18-23. The Creator made them *different but equal*: And, since God changes not, *He still SEES them EQUAL in Christ!* (Galatians 3:28) Moreover,...

Adam's body being made of dust, he was qualified to associate with all other creatures consisting of the same materials. Those unique-conditions placed mankind in the position of being the *official-liaison* between heaven and earth. The Creator authorized Adam (a term which designated women as well as men) to govern the planet for the Creator—*God had commanded Adam to exercise dominion over all the other creatures.* (Genesis 1:26-28, Psalms 8:3-8, Hebrews 2:5-9) *Man being God's highest-creature, he was BEST-qualified to hold that governing-position!* (And man is still authorized!) Furthermore,...

God having invested in Adam part of Himself, *Adam was imbued with God's very own righteous-nature*; just as Ecclesiastes 7:29 states: "God made man *UPRIGHT*, *BUT* they have sought out many [ungodly-]inventions." The fact that Christ *RESTORED* us to a righteous-state (2 Corinthians 5:21) confirms the fact that at the first, Adam was in perfect-right-standing with His Creator.

I must emphasize once again that Eve was invested with the same benefits and position as Adam regarding that Garden-Paradise. *Eve consisting of the very SAME material and spiritual-substance as Adam, whatever he was, she was!* If in any way Eve was *INFERIOR*, Adam had to be *INFERIOR* to that same degree. *ONLY* in their marriage-relationship was Adam to be *HEAD*. (Genesis 2:21-23, 5:1-2, 1 Corinthians 11:8-12) *Over the lower-creatures BOTH had authority!* (Incidentally, just as the head *NEEDS* the body to achieve things, the body also *NEEDS* the head for direction.) Back to fellowship,...

Religious-people think hobnobbing with God may be experienced only in the sweet-by-and-by (heaven); *and even then perhaps only by certain-worthy-saints.* So, it is no surprise that they cannot imagine Adam and Eve enjoying such benefits—and that on a daily-basis. Now if Adam and Eve did not, then we cannot. But, if Adam and Eve did, *Christians can experience such fellowship on this side of heaven!* (1 Corinthians 1:9, 1 John 1:3)

Adam and Eve being members of that Divine-family meant their having access to the family-treasures. *God made every material-thing Adam would need before He made Adam, and deposited all those good-things in the Garden of Eden—before He settled those man-creatures there.* (Genesis 2:8-15) And, *the goodies God gave man were not only for his survival; BUT for his enjoyment as well.* (Genesis 2:18-25) The same is still true. *God has planned for believers today MORE THAN mere survival. For just as the Creator BLESSED our original-ancestors with abundant-prosperity, so has He done for believers today!* (Genesis 1:29, Psalms 35:27, Malachi 3:10-11, 2 Corinthians 8:9, 9:8-10, 1 Timothy 4:8, 2 Peter 1:3, 3 John 2) So take courage in the Bible-Fact that,...

Man's Garden-Paradise lacked no goods or services; as is the case in so much of the modern-world. Nor did it lack beauty or any other pleasantry. In this modern-environment of dog-eat-dog, *prosperity for everybody is somewhat difficult for us to imagine. But, this-planet's-first-couple reveled in blessings on a daily-basis.* Plus, *the blessings required NO TOIL.* Toil did not exist until after Adam's fall. No sweat to get, and no tears or fears—just paradise—God's plan then, now and forever.

Every-good-thing was theirs for the plucking! Thus, their daily-schedule consisted not of hunting for game, gathering sticks for the fire, cooking meals, or washing dirty-dishes. Furthermore, there was no need for either antacids, or weight-control-diets. And not only that, in contrast to literally millions of laws people have to deal with today, *our first-ancestors had only ONE moral and legal-restriction.* (Genesis 2:15-17) Other than avoiding that lone-tree, no limits to enjoying the garden-goodies were placed on them, but their own appetites. Over the centuries, people have fantasized of discovering similar conditions somewhere on the earth; but I would advise the dreamers not to hold their breath while they wait— at least during this-present-age. *Heaven is not on earth yet!* But, more blessings are meant to be enjoyed by us who are *IN CHRIST* during this-age than most believers (due to religious-tradition) allow themselves to believe.

There was no sickness or disease in their world—No pain, sorrow, loss or death. In that paradise, before sin made its debut, they enjoyed perfect, peaceful, loving, living-conditions—and Jesus Christ came to this earth to *RESTORE* those conditions—many to be experienced in this-age, and on this-earth, before we get to heaven!

There was an enemy somewhere in God's universe, but as yet he had no leverage in that Garden-kingdom. Had Adam exercised his *God-given-authority,* the devil might still be roaming the vast expanses of space. (Job 1:7, 2:2, Luke 11:24) The moral of the story: Adam and Eve enjoyed Divine-Protection as long as they *OBEYED* God's Word. It still works like that! *Are you listening?*

Genesis 1:26-28 says that *God gave Adam authority over the earth and everything in it.* So Adam was God's helper in administering the affairs of the vast-universe; *the EARTH being Adam's POST.* Genesis 2:15: "And the Lord God took the man, and *PUT* him into the Garden of Eden to *DRESS* [till] it and to *KEEP* [guard] it." *There evidently existed some possible-THREAT to the Garden-Paradise; so in addition to commanding Adam to protect that piece of real-estate, God delegated full authority to Adam to keep it from falling into enemy-hands! So,...*

Authority was PART of Adam's benefit-package; and that authority was sufficient to safeguard the welfare of the earth and everything in it. When Jesus rebuked His disciples for failing to wield authority over that stormy-sea, *He was teaching them that even in their day, MAN STILL HAD THAT SAME AUTHORITY GOD GAVE ADAM at the beginning!* (Mark 4:39-41) Moreover, in order to operate legally on earth, *even our Savior had to use the very same authority God had delegated to Adam at the beginning.* (John 1:1, 14, 5:27, Hebrews 10:5) And,...

Scripture after Scripture proves beyond doubt that, *the Savior expects His followers to USE that God-given-authority over all the hostile-forces of nature, right up to His Second-Coming.* (Matthew 8:24-26, 28:18-20, Mark 16:17-18, Luke 6:40, John 14:12, 20:21-22) *The same authority given to Adam and Eve at the beginning is to be exercised by the church today; and is still effective in the world! Jesus commanded us to preach the Gospel to all the world in that ALL AUTHORITY IN HEAVEN AND EARTH WHICH HAD BEEN GIVEN TO HIM.* And neither the devil nor religion can reverse that command—*even though both have TRIED.* (Malachi 3:6, Matthew 24:35, 28:18-20, Hebrews 13:8) And all of that is why,...

To discover God's *present-day-plans* for Christians, in regard to physical, material, financial, and spiritual-benefits Adam and Eve enjoyed; and the authority they were given, we have to go back and investigate Adam's world to learn how it all started. *The truth is not all that complicated.* Rather, *it is the religious-falsehoods which have been drilled into the church over decades* (even for centuries), *and are circulating in MOST churches today, that have many Christians confused over those issues. Preachers have persuaded the church to believe almost every kind of doctrine which is CONTRARY TO Scripture concerning Christian-living.* When it comes to accurate-Bible-knowledge, it is hard to believe that we are living in an age of *mass-information and communication.* But, by focusing our attention on those blessings Adam and Eve enjoyed before their fall, we may catch a glimpse of the rich-blessings God has in mind for believers—even in this-age before Jesus returns. Mark 11:22-24 is still valid *TODAY! All things are possible to US who believe!*

Had our Creator not set the precedent with that first-human-couple, NONE of the goodies they enjoyed would be available today. And, our Creator has not altered His original-plans or purposes. (Malachi 3:6, Hebrews 13:8) *Jesus came to restore ALL that Adam lost!* (Luke 19:10)

So many believers have become so accustomed to all the miseries stemming from Adam's misdeed, that they are oblivious to the reality that the earth has not always existed in this present-state-of-disaster, and that those unplanned and undesirable-conditions will not continue forever. (2 Peter 3:3-13) *If we will redirect our attention from all that unpleasantness, and perceive things from God's-perspective (found only in God's Word), then our attitude about God's-purpose for us on earth NOW will be transformed. Christ commanded believers to go to all the world with good-news to a STRESSED-OUT, POOR, SICK, CONFUSED, AND DYING POPULATION.* (Matthew 9:35-38, 10:1, 7-8, 28:18-20, Mark 16:15-20, Acts 1:8) *Believers need to take on God's-view of everything; and both POSSESS THOSE SALVATION-blessings, and TELL OTHERS about those blessings being available to them!*

ONE CANNOT RESTORE WHAT HAS NOT EXISTED! Thus, the blessings Christ REINSTATED by His sacrifice upon the cross had to be part of God's original-creation. That Bible-Truth comprises a *MAJOR PORTION* of both the Bible itself; and the message of this unique-book.

What might this world be like today, had Adam and Eve not sinned? Sometimes, *I say to people facing a lot of paper-work connected to some business-transaction: "None of that would be necessary, had Adam and Eve only behaved themselves in the Garden of Eden!"* They had to tolerate no *RED-TAPE* in their daily-routine; but you and I have to face it constantly on account of their one blunder. Can you imagine living twenty-four-hours without facing hassle after hassle? Before our original-ancestors hooked up with the devil himself, Adam and Eve enjoyed a hassle-free-life. We believers too may live such a life (to some degree), *if we are willing to LEARN what the Bible teaches about the Christian-lifestyle!*

It cannot possibly be God's desire for ANY believer to SUFFER the pains and hardships so many people today have accepted as the norm even for believers. God does consider suffering persecution for our faithfulness to the Savior as normal (and even commendable) *on our part.* (2 Timothy 3:10-12, 1 Peter 2:18-23, 3:13-17, 4:12-16) However, *Christians suffering illness, poverty, damage from natural-disasters, or calamities resulting from sins we have not confessed, and forsaken, is neither normal nor commendable!* Our Savior bore those curses in our place on the cross. Christ destroyed our sins, diseases, curses and Satan's dominion over us. Jesus, therefore, expects us to resist *ALL* of those calamities! John 3:16, 2 Corinthians 8:9, Galatians 3:13-14, Colossians 1:13, James 4:7 and 1 Peter 2:24, 4:15, 5:8-9 *REVEAL THAT GOD NEVER PLANNED SUCH DISASTERS FOR MAN.*

Good as the news is that God has paid for salvation for EVERY human being living on the planet, only those who BELIEVE that good-news and openly acknowledge Jesus Christ as their Savior will receive salvation. Such demands are reasonable; because *HE WHO* purchased redemption for us has the right to set the *STANDARDS* for receiving the benefits thereof! Primary-standard,...

Obedience is KEY: As long as Adam and Eve obeyed God, they walked in creation-blessings. But when they disobeyed, they suffered the curses accompanying *SIN*. Isaiah 1:19: "If you are willing and *OBEDIENT*, you will eat the good things of the land." *That reveals God's will for His people both before Jesus came to earth and after Adam brought that curse on the human race!* Thus, we conclude that God desires blessings, not curses, in the lives of His obedient-people in every age and location!

Unfortunately, Adam and Eve believed Satan's lies, betraying God's trust; and forfeited the accompanying-blessings. Later in history, *that responsibility was LAID AT THE FEET of Israel; but they failed as well.* (Romans 2:24) *AND NOW*, according to Ephesians 3:10, the task of demonstrating God's goodness to the rest of creation has fallen upon the church. *So now it is up to you and me! What will our decision be?* We Christians now have the responsibilities Adam and Israel had; and more!

Prior to their treason, Adam and Eve had great-glory! Genesis 2:25: *"They were NAKED, but NOT ASHAMED."* Psalms 8:5: *"You made man a LITTLE LOWER than the angels [Hebrew—Elohim—god], and crowned him WITH GLORY and HONOR."* Jesus said He had come to *SAVE* what had been *LOST!* (Luke 19:10) *So it is tragic that so many believers today are AFFLICTED with humiliating-diseases, poverty and low-self-esteem.* But truth is,...

MANY of those tragedies are DUE to mind-numbing-religious-doctrines entrenched in the modern-church by deceived-preachers. Jeremiah 12:10: *"MANY PASTORS have DESTROYED My vineyard. They have trodden My people [Israel] under foot; and have made My pleasant-portion a desolate-wilderness." PASTORS! Same today!*

Christ encountered the same (but worse) conditions while He was on earth; *as the four-Gospels clearly bear out.* Jewish-religious-leaders repudiated every miracle He performed, and questioned every truth the Messiah preached. (Matthew 12:22-30) The very same response to miracles raises its ugly head in churches today! We often hear: "It is not God's will to work miracles today." And some even teach that God Himself afflicts His own people with sickness and poverty for some *mysterious-reason! Similar-demonic-teachings were rampant in the church early on* (Jude 3-4, etc); *and were prophesied to CONTINUE up to the very end of this-age!* (Mark 13:22, Acts 20:29-30, 2 Peter 2:1-3, 1 John 4:1-6) Especially in these modern-times, people believing and preaching the Bible-Truths Jesus *COMMANDED* us to preach and practice until His return *are branded heretics by many church-leaders; while they themselves teach powerless-religious-garbage to their congregations!* (Matthew 15:3, 28:20, Mark 7:6-8, 13, Colossians 2:8) That is why,...

Real-New-Testament-ministry being foreign to many denominations, it is no big surprise that many church-members are *MALNOURISHED* in spirit, soul and body. *Religious-traditions HAVE NO LIFE in them!* Only God's Living-Word can give believers a new nature, heal their body, reunite estranged-family-members, pay the bills, or solve any other human-problem. Jesus continues to perform miracles today, because that has been His will all along. Hebrews 13:8 is just as true today as ever!

Chapter Three

Restoration of the blessings

God changes NOT (Malachi 3:6, Hebrews 13:8); *NOR compromises His eternal-plans!* Thus, *the devil has NO CONTROL over ANY of God's redemptive-activities.* But, *he is the pusher of many so-called-Christian-doctrines.* God authorized no one to reverse the roles of the devil and the Godhead, nor mingle their characteristics; but the church-at-large has gotten Christ and the devil all mixed up as to the purposes and activities of each. Not satisfied with the mere *FALL* of man, the devil attacked man's spirit, soul, and body with every-kind of misery; and then *BLAMED GOD* for all those tragedies. What is even worse is that, the church has fallen for the devil's lies; incorporating them into their fundamental-beliefs; thus robbing many saints of many Gospel-blessings!

God created everything *GOOD*; including Adam and *ALL* his Eden-experiences. (Genesis 1:31) Later on God did acknowledge that *ONE* thing needed improvement: *Adam being companionless was not good for his future.* (Genesis 2:18) God *SOLVED* that problem by forming a whole new human being from Adam's body—God made woman out of man, and then joined her back to him in the *FIRST*-marriage. (Genesis 2:22, Matthew 19:6) *That placed woman in the same class with man—God saying so in* Genesis 5:2—*where He called them BOTH ADAM!*

Therefore, the woman had responsibility, along with man, in *BOTH tilling* and *guarding* the Garden of Eden. And, for a short-period-of-time, their Pristine-Paradise ran smoothly within the Divine-system. Because,...

Our wise-Creator purposely built into His universe a strict-orderliness. He designated a place for everything; then put everything in its place. Although many people are not comfortable with such precise-precision, *surely they appreciate the fact that they do not FLOAT off into outer space—gravity holding them on solid-ground.* The Master-Designer, *planning for creation to function in an orderly-manner, He has made ample-provision for all to be blessed by fitting into that Divine-arrangement.*

So How did this weird-world that we live in come to be in the first place—*considering that God originally set everything into motion the way He wanted it?* Scripture fills us in that, long ago, certain angelic-beings violated the *heavenly-precise-arrangements*; then spread those *DISRUPTIONS* to our planet. The *BASICS* of all that are recorded in Genesis 3:1-19, 6:1-8, Job 1:6-12, 2:1-7, Isaiah 14:12-15, Ezekiel 28:11-19, Matthew 25:41-46, Romans 5:12-17, 2 Corinthians 11:3-4, 2 Peter 2:4, 1 John 5:19, Jude 6-7, Revelation 12:9, 20:1-3—history of sin and its results in broad-biblical-perspective.

While many preachers emphasize the wrath of God on sinful-humanity from that day forward, *let us focus our attention on the redemptive-actions the Creator took in Eden before the sinners were expelled.* Not willing to forsake His original-plan for humanity, *the Creator put into action His pre-historically-drafted-redemption-plan before He meted out their judgment.* (Ephesians 1:4-14, 1 Peter 1:18-20, Revelation 13:8, etc., etc., etc.)

Having announced those redemptive-plans (Genesis 3:15), the Redeemer immediately set them into motion. His first-installment was His own sacrifice of innocent-animals *to cover the guilt of* those first-human-sinners. (Genesis 3:21) *God made the-first-leather-wardrobe!*

And removing those animals' skins meant shedding their blood and taking their life. *God Himself began the practice of shedding-innocent-blood to atone for sin!* We could say, then, that the first-blood-covenant *kicked in* before Adam and Eve were *kicked out* of that paradise! And, *that sort of sacrifice was necessary, until our Lord poured out His blood in behalf of EVERY earth-dweller.* (Acts 20:28, Hebrews 9:22-26, Revelation 1:5, etc.)

God did not overlook *human-rebellion*; but provided atonement for it. But, still, judgment was forthcoming: Sin had to be dealt with! Yet, God was more concerned about the sinner, than about sin itself. While sin could be atoned for, if man remained a sinner (sin-producer), there would be *NO END* to sin. *Adam's NEW-sin-nature caused all of his sin-sufferings. So God had to deal with mankind's SIN-NATURE, in order to restore man's right-standing with his Creator.* Thus, God never abandoned plan *A*—but put the redemptive-portion of plan *A* into operation to get plan *A* back on track. *NO PLAN B!*

In Genesis 3:15, God said He put enmity (adversity) between that Serpent's-seed and the woman's-*SEED*—Christ—And, that the woman's-*SEED* would eventually crush the Serpent's-head (authority); *meaning that God would not leave man in the-enemy's-camp.* The Creator esteemed the Adversary an unredeemable-entity, *while setting man's redemption into motion right on the spot!* In Galatians 3:16, *Paul said that prophecy of the SEED of Abraham referred to Christ. And, Christ was also the woman's-SEED; Who on the cross CRUSHED the devil's head* (illegal-authority over the fallen-human-race)!

God's redemptive-promises were made good through Jesus Christ—the woman's-Seed—being found ONLY in Him. "*FOR, ALL THE PROMISES OF GOD IN HIM* [Jesus]

ARE YES; AND IN HIM AMEN [SO BE IT]." (2 Corinthians 1:20) *Only through faith in Christ's cross-sacrifice may we tap into those promises.* Moreover, *the promises are IN HIM, but they are unto the glory of God by believers; and cannot be fulfilled without believers. To whom else would God give cross-bought-blessings? And, getting in Christ is one of those blessings!* (Mark 16:16) Yet,...

There are also promises of judgment: *And one must consciously do nothing to QUALIFY for Divine-judgment*: Outside Christ judgment prevails! (John 3:18, 36) And, according to Matthew 21:21-22, Mark 11:22-24, John 15:7-8, Romans 10:9-10, Hebrews 10:36, James 1:5-7, and 1 John 3:22, *to gain Kingdom-blessings, one must exercise the Kingdom-principles of faith and obedience: Unwavering-faith in God's promises and unquestioned-obedience to all of His commands. And, even though the consequences of rebellion are eternally-unpleasant, God has altered neither His promises of judgment on rebels; nor His promises of salvation for REPENTANT-rebels.*

Christ's work on the cross was not the RESTITUTION OF ALL THINGS Peter prophesied about in Acts 3:21. Of course, *that future-event will certainly be dependent on Christ's cross-sacrifice!* However, *while waiting on that RESTITUTION of all things to occur in the future, Christ is presently building His CHURCH.* (Matthew 16:18)

How is the church to *AFFECT* people on earth? *And how does God EXPECT people to respond to the Gospel it preaches?* "Repent, and be converted [born-anew, or, from-above], *that your sins may be blotted out* [washed away by that shed-blood of Jesus]; *Whom heaven must keep in waiting, until the restitution of all things, which God spoke through the mouth of His holy prophets since the world began.*" (Acts 3:19-21) Therefore,...

THE FULFILLMENT OF THAT PROMISE MUST STILL BE FUTURE TO OUR DAY. Earthlings fare not well now, but when those conditions PREVAIL on the New-Earth, CURSES will PREVAIL nowhere on it—even though the center of the earth will be a place of torment for all who have not been born again. (Isaiah 66:22-24, Mark 9:42-48, Revelation 21:8) Present-world-conditions,...

There is a world-of-hurt around us today. And, that *HURT WILL NOT GO AWAY BEFORE JESUS RETURNS. Yet, believers are not required to participate in MOST of those miseries. Because of our SPIRITUAL-UNION WITH CHRIST, we are SPARED much of the suffering suffered by those NOT IN SPIRITUAL-UNION WITH CHRIST!*

The primary-purpose of this volume is to direct the Christian's attention to the countless-blessings already belonging to us during the present-age. Although there will be a perfect-world again sometime in the future, in which all things will be restored; *MANY* cross-blessings are available today—which *MANY* believers are missing out on today because of the *MANY* erroneous-religious-traditions entrenched in *MANY* churches today. Let us lay hold of present-day-cross-blessings, while we await the unimaginable-blessings of those ages to come.

Revelation 20:7-15 informs us that after God brings the devil's activities on this planet to a screeching-halt, He will settle *ALL* accounts with those who have served God's-adversary, from the first-transgression in heaven unto that final-judgment-day—be they angels, demons or men—Satan himself having already been cast into the Lake of Fire. While many seem to believe God is either oblivious to all earthly-events, or simply does not care, Scripture informs us God keeps records on everybody's attitudes, words, and actions. *None shunned!*

Revelation 21:4 *prophesies that in the NEW-EARTH* "*God will wipe away all tears from their eyes; and there will be no more death, sorrow, crying, or pain.*" Edenic-blessings will return to this renovated-earth. *No kind of evil will show up in that Eternal-Kingdom.* (Daniel 2:44, Revelation 21:7-8, 27) ALL curses will be removed from that realm. (Revelation 22:3) *Only creatures confined to that Lake of Fire for rebellion against the Creator will be doing any suffering.* (Isaiah 66:22-24, 2 Thessalonians 2:10-12, Revelation 20:10-15, 22:14-15) At present,...

Many daydream about how it will be SOMEDAY, but the Lord MADE IT POSSIBLE for us to experience many blessings in the-here-and-now! (Matthew 17:20, 18:18, Mark 11:23, John 15:7) I will cover some of those rich-realities in the latter-half of this book; *but NOW I must lay the foundation for a biblical-understanding of those New-Covenant-blessings—many of which are available to believers even during this-evil-age.*

In order to fully-fathom future-world-conditions after God CHANGES present-world-conditions, we needed to become fully-familiar with man's perfect-world. But, *we must now grasp the significance of that transgression in Eden, in order to comprehend the depth of our-Savior's-sacrifice in behalf of the human race. Both man and his world deteriorated upon his joining the-devil's-rebellion.* What really happened when Adam and Eve sinned?

Chapter Four

Adam united with Satan

To fully-understand the tragedy, which befell Adam and Eve (*and through them every human being existing after them*) through their one-blunder in their Garden-Paradise, we have to take seriously the prohibition God made in Genesis 2:17—*which Adam and Eve obviously DID NOT take seriously! Modern-man's not-very-bright-tendency to pay little or no HEED to the Creator's strict-warnings can be TRACED all the way back to that first-couple in their Eden-setting.* Were God's instructions to them confusing? Could He have made His warning any clearer? *What part of no did Adam not understand?* "Of the *TREE* of the knowledge of good and evil *YOU MUST NOT EAT!* For, in the day you eat it, you will surely *DIE* [literally, *DYING* you *WILL DIE*]." *People today owe their foolish-behavior-patterns to their undeniable-connection to those first-human-transgressors.* That does not clear modern-transgressors from *BLAME* for their own sins, however. Romans 5:12: "Through one man [Adam], sin entered the world, and death came in through sin, *and so death spread to all men; because all sinned.*" Adam's nature having been altered, his offspring had the same *PERVERTED-NATURE* as *PERVERTED-ADAM* had. Man having been created to bring forth after his *OWN KIND*; and his *OWN KIND* now being the sinful-kind, his new-nature coming from his spiritual-union with the devil, Adam's offspring were tied to the devil too! But,...

WHAT POWER existed back then that could possibly overcome the WORD of Him, Who had brought all things into being by His WORD? (John 1:1-3, Hebrews 11:3)

What being had ability to conquer those two-perfect-specimens of GOD'S-CREATIVE-GENIUS? Was Satan so strong and those humans so weak that they had little or no choice in the matter? Did some foreign-power come to that garden and take it over—or was the fall a matter of treason on man's part? We learn the actual-truth about that and other issues concerning human-life only by an unbiased-search through Scripture for answers to such valid-questions. (2 Peter 1:2-4) One valid-answer is,...

Mere SURFACE-SCANNING of Scripture produces no honest-answers to our questions. SURFACE-SCANNING being a sure-sign of LAZINESS on the part of SURFACE-SCANNERS, AND LAZINESS BEING ERROR, SURFACE-SCANNERS ARE OBVIOUSLY ERROR-PRONE! Gaining Bible-Truth without distorting it DEMANDS DILIGENCE! (Jeremiah 29:13, 2 Timothy 2:15, 2 Peter 1:5-11)

The truth is that Adam and Eve rejected God's Word outright! Genesis 3:6 proves that *Eve placed GREATER-VALUE on the-devil's-appealing-words than upon God's clear-warning.* But Adam did no better. He watched his wife make that thoughtless-decision without a protest. "She did eat, then gave also to her husband WITH HER [in the same place at the same time]; and HE also ate." Scripture establishes that Adam was not deceived, but just went along with Eve's deranged-decision. (Genesis 3:13, 1 Timothy 2:14) Eve was deceived; *BUT humanity FELL in Adam.* In those days, Adam and Eve were all of mankind that existed, so it was their sin that filled this world with curses. But let us research further, to learn some pre-history that prepped the garden-tragedy.

An accurate-understanding of the Garden-Paradise-Fiasco necessitates an investigation into the devil's own fall—including accurate-biblical-truth about his ORIGIN, his DEPARTURE from his Creator's original-plan for him and the devil's PRESENT-PURPOSES and STRATEGIES. In other words, *to understand Satan's-PART in human-history we must learn all about the-devil's-own-history!* Otherwise, *we will be unable to grasp the full import of that Eden-tragedy.* The rest of this chapter unfolds the Bible-Account of *Satan's origin, his fall, and how those pre-historical-events affected humankind.* Chapters-five and six reveal Satan's *selfish-purposes,* and expose his *evil-tactics* in *this-evil-age.* (Most-essential-revelation!)

The angelic-being originally named Lucifer, through rebellion, became the devil, Satan, Adversary, Serpent, Tempter, Accuser, Great Red Dragon, god-of-this-age, and The-Wicked-One. Such telling-titles alert us to the devil's character and designs. Moreover, *Bible-accounts of Satan's atrocities are conclusive-evidence that*—every human-predicament is connected to the fallen-Lucifer; plus man's unwise-decision to fall for his deceptions!

First Timothy 3:6 reveals that the devil fell from his original-God-given-position. *That verse falls right in the midst of Paul's-list-of-qualifications-for-church-leaders*; where Paul made it clear it was unwise to put a novice (*A NEW-CONVERT* to the Christian-faith) in leadership-positions: "Lest being lifted up with *PRIDE,* [that novice might] fall into the *condemnation of the devil."* Paul did not suggest that Satan would condemn the novice, but that the untrained-Christian might fall under the same condemnation Lucifer once did because of his *PRIDE.*

Now, *the devil will attempt to bring Christians under condemnation, but he has no legal-right to do so.* (John 8:44, 12:31, 16:8-11) *He accuses, but has no authority to condemn!* (1 Peter 5:8, Revelation 12:10) *If the devil could condemn believers, it would not matter if we were NOVICES in the faith or SEASONED-VETERANS OF THE*

CHRISTIAN-FAITH; he would try to take us down. Thus, it is obvious Paul was not suggesting new-converts might incur Satan's-wrath: *All believers face that from time to time!* No, Paul was warning those church-leaders that new-converts are more likely to be lifted up in pride, so place themselves under *Divine-condemnation*—just like Lucifer did in antiquity. More than one New Testament version unveils that shade of meaning of the Greek in that passage. Most are clear by their English-rendering that Satan is a fallen-creature. That means he was not created *EVIL!* Sometime after Lucifer was brought into being he decided to go astray; and when he realized he was condemned, with no hope of recovery, he began to spread his rebellion to *ALL THE REST* of this universe; inflicting as much damage on creation as he possibly could. His connivance upon this planet has negatively-affected all mankind to this day! Continuing,...

As controversial as numerous-theologians consider them to be, the two Scripture passages, which present the actual *FACTS* of Lucifer's *pre-history-fall* are Isaiah 14:12-15 and Ezekiel 28:11-19. *The FACTS recorded in those two passages could not in any way apply to any human being.* No *MAN* has ever *ASCENDED TO* heaven (by his own power); nor *FALLEN FROM* heaven. (A man would have to be located in a place before he could fall from it.) The *BEING* Isaiah referred to must have been *OTHER THAN HUMAN!* Some scholars contend that the entire-twenty-eighth-chapter of Ezekiel refers to Adam back in Eden; but all of their arguments break down in light of the contents of that chapter itself! Ezekiel 28:1-10 *does refer to a human being; and even uses the term Adam.* However, throughout the Old Testament, Adam sometimes refers to the human race in general, as well as to certain members of it; and not always to the first-Adam. Now Ezekiel 28:1-10 does tell about the *PRINCE*

OF TYRUS who contented that he was a god. Of course, the Living-God will not tolerate such talk from those in leadership-positions. (Acts 12:21-24) God assured that Tyrus-Prince that due to his blasphemy he would die a horrible-death *at the hands of men*; not at the hands of God. So that prince was definitely a man—not a god.

But, Ezekiel 28:11-19 addresses a being altogether different from the *PRINCE* of Tyrus—the *KING* of Tyrus. Ezekiel used another Hebrew word for that potentate—the most common word for king in the Old Testament; meaning *LOFTY-ONE*. *The King of Tyrus could not have been Adam, nor any other human being!* For one thing, *the King of Tyrus is never referred to as ADAM in those-nine-verses.* Second, *that king had superhuman-traits.* Moreover, that king had been created—not born. Adam was *THE ONLY* human being God had directly-created. Everyone else sprang either directly from Adam, or was born of one of Adam's offspring. *Ezekiel's description of the King of Tyrus does have some surface-similarities to Adam's Eden-experiences; so, many theologians CLAIM Ezekiel was referring to Adam in that passage.* Ezekiel, however, tagged that being a *CHERUB*; which the Bible never uses in connection with human beings—*NEVER!*

In addition, the *KING* of Tyrus had engaged in *much trading—making deals—picturing ON-GOING-ACTIVITY*; whereas Adam got into trouble by committing only one sin! That unique being was also *lifted up* on account of his *beauty*. But, when was that ever said about Adam? *He had even been cast down from the mountain of God, whereas there is no mention of a mountain of God in the Eden-account.* Plus, God humiliated that King of Tyrus before other kings! What kind of kings existed on earth in Adam's day? That part of Ezekiel's vision referred to Satan—*the evil-personality behind all of the evil-actions of the earthly-Prince-of-Tyrus!* See John 8:44 again.

Those who reject the truth that Isaiah-fourteen and Ezekiel-twenty-eight refer to the devil himself obviously believe that God created the devil in his evil-state right from the start—implying that the devil was God's idea.

Why is John 8:44 important? *It is the biblical-key to understanding mankind's connection to his own enemy!* Jesus said to some *unbelieving*-Jews: "You are *OF* your [spiritual-]father, the devil, and the lusts of your father *YOU* will do. He was a murderer from the beginning [of his rebellion; *NOT* from the beginning of his existence], and abode not in the truth [God's Word—John 17:17], because there is no truth [Word of God] in him [Satan]. When he speaks a lie he speaks of his own [resources]: For he is a liar, and the father of lies." But,...

When did Satan become mankind's spiritual-father? The day Adam SINNED! Every-living-creature had been created to reproduce after its own kind; *and Adam had no offspring until after he became the sinful-kind! Thus, that unholy-alliance between man and Satan originated with Adam—not later with any of Adam's descendants. Sinful-mankind has one-common-progenitor—the Adam who rebelled against his Creator. Through Adam, Satan became "the-god-of-this-age."* (2 Corinthians 4:4)

John 8:34 holds another key to understanding the-pitiful-human-condition after Adam. *"Whoever commits sin is THE SERVANT of sin."* Adam and Eve were God's servants before they sinned by rejecting God's warning about that tree, and believing Satan's words—by which they *BECAME* servants (even the children) of the devil. (Matthew 13:38, John 8:38-44, 1 John 3:10, 5:19)

BY THAT TREASONOUS-ACT Adam and Eve passed from life to death (Romans 5:12, 1 Corinthians 15:22); *so people now need to be transformed from death to life.* (John 5:24, 2 Corinthians 5:17, 1 John 3:14)

Therefore, God is *NOT* everyone's *Spiritual-Father!* In John 8:44, the Lord said: "You are of your father the devil." *Jesus was not implying the devil had created his own human race.* For, the devil has never created anything! Matthew 22:32 says *God is not the God of the dead, but of the living. God is Creator and Judge of ALL men, but not their Father!* Did He not offer to *BECOME GOD* to Abram? (Genesis 17:7) Who was Abram's god before that day? Satan is identified as the "god-of-this-age" (2 Corinthians 4:4), and Abram was in that system until God called him out of it. (Joshua 24:2)

John 8:34 says those who practice sin on a regular basis do so for a reason—*They are enslaved to it!* They are imprisoned by an evil they can by no means deliver themselves from. Who is the culprit behind their sins? The devil! (1 John 3:8) So, *bondage to sin is bondage to the devil; which is what Jesus proclaimed to and about the-whole-Jewish-nation.* Yet, they naturally disagreed. However, the same flaw flourishes among the Gentiles. (Romans 11:32, Galatians 3:22, 1 John 5:19)

Romans 6:16 reinforces that truth: "Know you not, *that to whom you yield yourselves servants to obey, his servants you are to whom you obey*; whether of *sin* [the devil] unto death, or of *obedience* unto righteousness?" Notice the emphasis on obedience. Whoever Adam and Eve obeyed, that person would be their master. *As long as they obeyed the Creator He was their God; but when they rebelled by believing Satan, they exchanged lords.* How did Satan become the-god-of-this-world? Through the *disobedience* of Adam and Eve! Romans 6:22 says we are made free from sin by applying Christ's blood to our lives; *and so we become God's servants once again.* Sin being the *VERY OPPOSITE* of obedience to God, sin was what made Adam and Eve servants of Satan!

Second Peter 2:19 concurs: *"By the one a person is overcome, to the same one* [the overcoming-one] *is he or she brought into bondage." Adam and Eve having been created to REPRODUCE their own kind; their sin having made them the sinful-kind; putting them under bondage to Satan; their offspring were under that same bondage.* (Romans 5:12-19) *Jesus Christ is the only escape from mankind's CONNECTION to sinful-Adam—who through sin BECAME IDENTIFIED WITH THE DEVIL HIMSELF—God's-adversary! Sinners are God's adversaries.*

Consider the connection of the words *commit, yield to, obey,* and *be overcome by.* How did Satan overcome Adam and Eve? By deceiving them, he persuaded them to *commit sin, yield to, and obey him!* In so doing, they were *overcome* by him. How does one yield to the devil? *By trusting in and heeding his words!* But, how did the devil convince that couple *TO ACT* upon his words? *By promising them goodies THAT SOUNDED BETTER than those God had provided! DECEPTIVE-PROMISES!*

Earth's-first-human-beings *faced two-opposing-sets of demanding-words* (just like it is today); *which thrust them into an awkward-position. Not being able to travel in opposite directions at the same time, they CHOSE the path that SEEMED to be in their best interest.* (Proverbs 14:12, 16:25) Satan's words diametrically-opposed the Creator's-clear-warning. And, Eve placed confidence in the Serpent's-words instead of the Divine-prohibition—and then acted accordingly. Actions always manifest in either obedience or disobedience to an appealing-voice: Whichever voice has the greatest appeal. Thus,...

Only those who obey God's Words are *HIS*-children. Everyone else remains under the devil's-dominion! The Lord explained in John 8:47 *how one becomes joined to*

God and released from Satanic-lies. "The one who is of God *hears* God's words: You, therefore, *hear* them not, because, you are not of God." The Greek word for *hear* means to HEAR WITH INTENT TO OBEY what is heard. Those Jews obviously did not want to OBEY what they had HEARD Jesus say. When one is blinded by Satan's lies, he or she is unable to perceive the truths of God's Word. *However, when a person DECIDES to believe and heed God's Word, he or she will discard demonic-lies in favor of Divine-Truth.* (Always a wise-decision!)

Authoritative-words released by a convincing-figure demands a response from the hearer. God commanded Adam and Eve to shun that *one forbidden tree*, and He expected them to obey Him explicitly. *To obey God is to ACT IN LINE WITH His commands!* Had Adam and Eve done as they were *TOLD*, they would have steered clear of trouble for both them and their posterity. *In order to test their loyalty*, however, *God had to allow the devil to present them with opposing-possibilities*; to which they had to respond. Man was faced with his first-decision; and biblical-history reveals that he made a-poor-one!

Obeying God and resisting the devil is the only safe-and-sane-road-to-travel. Disrespecting the Divine-order invites everything to fall apart—which is what occurred in Adam's world—and which continues in this world to this day! *To heed the-devil's-suggestions is to heed lies; which become detrimental to the welfare of the heeder.* The devil's words are death-words; having sprung from a-spiritually-*DEAD*-angel. *To act in line with the devil's deception is to cooperate with a destroyer to bring about one's very own destruction! Life residing in God's-Word, ONLY those who obey His Word experience REAL-LIFE.* (Proverbs 4:20-22, Matthew 4:3-4, John 6:63, 8:31-32, James 4:7-8, 1 Peter 5:6-10, 1 John 3:8, 4:4, 5:9-12) Wrapping it up,...

We *NOW* understand *HOW* and *WHY* Adam and Eve got separated from God and united with the devil: *How and why they FELL from having some control over their life to getting the RAW-END of their new-deal the rest of their life*—Deuteronomy 28:44. *Deliberately-disobeying God's-warning on one hand and heeding the devil's-lies on the other, Adam and Eve separated themselves from Him Who alone possesses and gives life; and hooked up with him who can only produce death. And it works the SAME OLD WAY TODAY—because multitudes still make the-same-old-unwise-decisions today! And on a regular basis!* Not too smart on man's part—but it is history.

In the next chapter, we learn about Satan's *purpose* in spreading rebellion into the earth-realm; and look at God's reason for permitting such to occur in our world. The truths contained therein are real eye-openers, and will greatly increase the readers' biblical-weaponry.

Chapter Five

Satan's-evil-designs

Significant-STUDIES by qualified-Bible-scholars into Satan's-EVIL-DESIGNS are rare. And as a result; many church-members assert things about the devil which are biblically-inaccurate and destructive to the thoughtless-talebearers. Erroneous-views and ideas about the devil prevail in religious-minds; attributing to the devil MORE power than he actually possesses. Hence, the necessity for believers to become familiar with how Satan thinks! If we can get into his mind, we can anticipate his every move: And with such Bible-knowledge under our belts, we can render the devil's attacks against us ineffective! *Seasoned-military-leaders have learned the importance of knowing HOW the enemy THINKS. And, Paul warned Corinthian-believers and us against being IGNORANT of the devil's-deceptive-devices.* (2 Corinthians 2:11)

The Bible teaches us about the *mad-but-calculated-reasoning behind the-devil's-every-action.* John 10:10: "The thief comes not, except to *steal, kill,* and *destroy." That statement is universally-recognized as speaking of the devil.* People will mimic either God or the devil; and our Savior *PURPOSES* neither to steal, kill nor destroy. (Ezekiel 18:23, 32, Luke 9:56, 2 Peter 3:9) Thus, *liars, thieves, murderers, and destroyers MUST get their evil-nature from Satan! In the-entire-universe, there are only TWO-sources of personality-qualities*: Our Creator, *Who evokes beneficial-behavior, and Satan who spawns all-kinds-of-evil!* (Jeremiah 29:11, Galatians 5:7-8, James 1:16-17, 3:14-17) *The devil is the chief-thief, chief-liar, chief-murderer, chief-pervert and chief-destroyer.*

Barring the unsolicited-aid of Satan, human beings could not have committed all of the *diabolical-atrocities* occurring on the earth; *nor stooped so low in character.* (Ephesians 2:2, 1 John 5:19) So not all of our thoughts or actions are birthed from our humanity. *EITHER God or SATAN is the primary-influence in the life of EVERY being in this universe. Satan cannot create personality; but he perverts every personality he has influence over. All creation was made GOOD in the beginning, but later became polluted. Satan was the first self-deluded-and-polluted-being; and his diabolical-design has been, and still is, to contaminate all the rest of creation, just as he contaminated himself—so that God, IN JUDGMENT, will destroy it all.* But God's plan smashes the devil's plan!

However, *merely knowing the fact that Satan steals, kills and destroys in not enough to ward off his attacks. We must also know the reasons behind his maneuvers.* In the field of *LAW*, uncovering a criminal's motivation is a major-factor in unraveling legal-cases. *That is just as true in dealing with our spiritual-adversary the devil.* If people are convinced the devil is only an impersonal-force, they will *RESPOND* to him accordingly. However, finding out that the devil is a created-being, which has emotions, intelligence and an eternal-destiny, they will know that they have to deal with him much-differently. *Bible-knowledge of Satan's character-traits exposes his mode-of-operation; enabling Christians to recognize his connection to every-evil-situation.* Christ, Peter, James, John and Paul *ALL* warned us Christians to *NEVER* be caught off guard by Satan. (Mark 14:38, 1 Corinthians 10:13, Ephesians 4:27, James 4:7-8, 1 Peter 5:8-9, 1 John 5:18, Revelation 3:10) Does Scripture record the devil's emotional-displays? Revelation 12:12 provides a snapshot of *HIS OUTRAGE* (emotional-response to one of his defeats) against the Jews in an event yet future:

"*WOE* to the inhabitants of earth, and sea! For, the devil is come down to you, *having great wrath*, because he knows he has only a short time." That verse proves that Satan has *emotions*, that he is an *intelligent-being* and *faces a not-so-good-eternal-destiny*. First Peter 5:8 tells us *he purposely SEEKS those he may devour. That reveals the devil's animosity toward all of creation; also proving Satan's vengeance against God for his own fall. Animosity and vengeance are both negative-emotions—* one-more-vital-piece-of-information about our enemy.

Moreover, *the legion of demons Jesus cast out of the Gadarene-demoniac expressed horror at the thought of having to VACATE their human-habitat—and evidenced their knowledge of having a fate-of-TORMENT*—starting sometime in the future. (Luke 8:26-33) In the Matthew account of that incident, the demons begged Jesus not to torment them *BEFORE* that time. (Matthew 8:28-32) Although they were demons, and not the devil himself, *they betrayed their connection to the devil by exhibiting negative-emotions, and knowing about their future-fate-of-torment.* Luke 13:11-16 *connects demonic-activity to the devil—AND the connection of demons to sickness.*

In John 8:44, Christ said to some Jews: "You are of your father the devil, *and the LUSTS of your father YOU WILL TO DO." If LUST is a negative-emotion in humans, and humans get it from the devil, it must be a negative-emotion in the devil!* Proven in Luke 22:31: "Jesus said: 'Simon, Simon, *Satan HAS DESIRED* [emotion] *to have you, so that he may sift* [put pressure on] *you just like* [people do] *wheat.'" The devil has ONLY evil-desires!*

Hate is also a *prominent-people-problem*; yet people inherit their *hateful-nature* from the devil! In John 7:7, Jesus stated: "*The world cannot hate you* [people of the world], *but Me it hates because I testify about it that the works thereof are EVIL." They desired to do the lusts of their father the devil!* (John 8:44) *The lost hated Christ because their mind was aligned with His enemy, Satan.* Lost people express animosity against all that is Godly, because: "The-god-of-this-world (Satan—2 Corinthians 4:4)," "The prince of the power of the air; *the spirit that now WORKS in the children of disobedience* (Ephesians 2:2)," fills them with *HATE.* Satan is the spiritual-force behind all-evil-human-hatred! See Ephesians 6:12.

What about *PRIDE?* Is pride unique to humanity; *or did people inherit pride from some other source?* Where did pride originate? Isaiah 14:12-15 says that Lucifer, by his *SELF-GENERATED-PRIDE* became the adversary of Almighty God. *PRIDE* is one earmark of this present-evil-age (1 John 2:16), and 2 Corinthians 4:4 says that the devil is the "god-of-this-age." Believers are warned in 1 Timothy 3:6 against being lifted up *WITH PRIDE*— the *CAUSE* of Lucifer's own downfall. That tells us,...

The devil and his demonic-cohorts are personalities that possess a-full-range-of-emotions—albeit negative-ones. They all display and spawn *lust, fear, hate, rage,* and *pride. They also have super-intelligence; which we cannot overcome by human-power and intellect.* It takes Godly-wisdom and power to defeat Satan and his crew. (Psalms 119:98, Proverbs 3:5, 1 Corinthians 1:25) *The devil and his angelic and demonic-rebels being doomed to eternal-torment, they are obviously moral-beings that are God's arch-enemies.* (Matthew 8:29, 25:41, 2 Peter 2:4-9, Jude 6-7) So now this question may arise,...

WHY did the devil become the *ENEMY* of humanity? What got him so upset in the first place? Why is he out to destroy all creation and to blaspheme God's name in the process? Only God and the *former-Lucifer* know his original-intent for rebelling against his Creator's rules, but the Bible-account of his fall provides vital-insights into the devil's present-day-motivations and designs.

An UNSUCCESSFUL-attempt of a criminal to achieve some ILLEGAL-objective almost always hurls him into a selfish-rage over his FAILURE to beat the legal-system. Since the criminal can count on *no-legal-backing* from *authorized-authorities*, he must be *shrewd* and *sneaky* before, during and after his action. *Although he knows any illegal-move is a GAMBLE, when the establishment beats him, he FEELS unbearable-humiliation, and takes on a victim-mentality. Humiliation is a negative-emotion that cannot be tolerated by those lifted up in pride. They feel that they must save face* (vindicate themselves and their selfish-illegal-actions) *by harboring hatred toward the system that beat them; and by swearing vengeance against it*—the trap Lucifer set for himself and then fell headlong into back in the *pre-historical-eons. Failing in his ambitious-attempt to conquer God and take over the universe,* Lucifer swore vengeance against his very own Creator, and became His *ADVERSARY* (enemy of God—Satan and the devil—Revelation 20:1-2)! Thus,...

Without doubt, *the lost get their evil-tendencies from the devil, their spiritual-father.* (John 8:44) *Satan is the instigator of the tantrums people publicly-display, when they become ENRAGED over their failure at outsmarting God.* Isaiah 14:12-15, Ezekiel 28:11-19, John 8:44 and Revelation 12:9-12 *prove that RASH-human-behavior is ROOTED in Satan's temper-tantrums over his failures.*

That Archangel-Lucifer, and one third of the angels, made an all-out-attempt to dethrone the Creator of the universe and usurp the awesome-authority, which God alone had wisdom and ability to wield. If such were not so, Isaiah 14:12-15 and Ezekiel 28:11-19 would make no sense—*for those two passages cannot possibly refer to any other created-being.* Lucifer became Satan!

BUT, Satan being one of God's creatures, *we KNOW that he had not always existed as an evil-being—SINCE GOD CREATED EVERYTHING GOOD! EVIL sprang forth AFTER the original-creation; AND ORIGINATED FROM A SOURCE OTHER THAN THE CREATOR!* (Genesis 1:31, Ezekiel 28:14-16) Thus, the Creator cannot possibly be the author of evil. And neither is humankind, because; *although humankind is steeped in evil, we know that a FALLEN-BEING existed in this universe BEFORE Adam and Eve were created. It is evident that LUCIFER—who became the devil and Satan—was THE FIRST to commit evil—and is the ultimate-source of all evil.* (1 John 3:8)

Satan became furious over the trouble he incurred when he *SEPARATED HIMSELF FROM HIS CREATOR— And Scripture clearly teaches that Satan can never right that wrong—and that he is well-aware of his deserved-condemnation because of that rebellion.* (Matthew 8:29, John 12:31, 16:8-11, Revelation 12:12) Therefore,...

What would our Adversary have left to gain (or lose) by continuing that rebellion? For him, it was a case of gaining all or losing everything; and by taking that risk Lucifer lost everything. Then, God created a new-being called man; giving him authority Lucifer had *FAILED* to obtain through rebellion. Consequently, the devil hates all mankind with a passion; and is the most miserable of all God's creatures! *NO PEACE for the wicked!*

Whereas many believe the primary-personality-flaw of mankind is lying, *I have observed in infants another character-trait which manifests itself long before infants are developed enough to start LYING: Selfishness!* Even *ADULTS* who endeavor to be honest at all times tend to display the very *same-ungodly-inclination* at times. Yet, *although human-friction stems from human-selfishness, Satan is the ultimate-instigator of ALL human-atrocities.* Humanity is selfish, because of its spiritual-union with selfish-Satan! (John 8:44, Ephesians 6:11-17) Yet,...

Selfishness is not confined to the devil and sinners. That demonic-trait runs rampant within the church as much as it does anywhere else on earth. In fact, *recent studies prove that the divorce-rate among Christians is roughly the same as it is in the lost-world—and divorce is the result of one or both spouses being SELFISH! And friction between church-denominations is from the same evil-source!* (1 Corinthians 1:10-13, James 3:14-16)

By God giving man earthly-dominion, which Lucifer had failed to gain through rebellion, He added insult to Lucifer's injury. Moreover, *the Creator made man in His own IMAGE.* (Genesis 1:26-28) Infuriated by that move of the Creator, *Satan set out to destroy the human race; his up-front-plan being to infect humanity with his own selfish-nature; and thus bring upon humanity the same CONDEMNATION Lucifer had brought upon himself!* The Serpent had promised Eve that by her partaking of the forbidden tree: *"You will be like god."* (Genesis 3:5) Had Lucifer not set for himself that same goal? *Considering that a similar-act had backfired on Lucifer, why was he trying to talk humans into doing the same-stupid-thing?* Answer: Hating both God and humanity as he did, *the devil attempted to remake mankind in his* (Satan's) *very own image!* His nature now being selfish, *the devil was trying to refashion human beings into selfish-creatures*; so that they would become objects of God's wrath, just as Lucifer had become. And man fell into that trap.

The Evil-One *KNOWS* that he cannot be redeemed: His good-old-days are long-gone. Satan's only incentive for continuing his rebellion is *TO DESTROY* as much of creation as he possibly can, and make his Creator look *BAD* in the process. Although his maneuvers are futile, as far as his own future is concerned, he is still trying to be like the-Most-High—only in a destructive-sense.

The concept of reshaping human beings into Satan's evil-image is obvious in some English-versions of Hosea 9:10. The last sentence in that verse reveals the tragic-truth that *idol-worshipers become LIKE the detestable-thing they worship. The devil's-dupes take on his image and likeness!* Is that not what the Lord meant in John 8:44, where He said that *men lust with the same lusts as their spiritual-father, the devil? Working in the sons of disobedience, is he not mirroring himself in their evil, selfish-actions?* (Ephesians 2:2) So we must ask,...

What is the devil's purpose in reshaping people into the likeness of God's-enemy? The prince of this fallen-world having already been *JUDGED AND CONDEMNED* (John 12:31), *every being united with him will incur the same judgment! Humanity IS LURED INTO worshipping everything the-god-of-this-age parades before its eyes.* (1 John 2:15-17) *And even though most folks know not they are serving the devil by chasing after those things, they are SERVING him nonetheless; and he knows that will be their downfall! The-devil's-demonic-design!*

An example of that is seen in Numbers 25:1-18 and Revelation 2:14. In Numbers twenty-three and twenty-four we see God thwarting Balaam's-attempt to place a curse on Israel. *God protected HIS COVENANT-PEOPLE from the dark-forces at work in that false-prophet while they were compliant with the Covenant-commands. But, some of the Jewish-leaders PUT themselves UNDER the curse by committing adultery with the Moabite women. When they transgressed God's Covenant-regulations, to enjoy selfish-carnal-pleasure, they removed themselves from that Covenant-protection.* The same is true today!

Looking deeper into the subject of human-hatred: *It is amazing how soon unsaved-people come to hate their once-good-friends, when those friends turn to Christ for salvation! Lost-people do not have to be trained to hate believers: The hate is immediate and automatic!* (John 15:18-21) Verse-nineteen informs us: "If you were of [belonged to] the world, the world would love you as its own: *But,* you are not of the world, because I have chosen [delivered] you out of this world. Thus, the world hates you." Lost people have *NO* rational reason to hate Christians—they just do! In John 7:7, *Jesus revealed the key to that mystery—saying the world hated Him for exposing its evil works.*

How did the Lord expose those evil-works? With the Word of God! That is *WHY* this world *HATES genuine-Christians.* In the Lord's prayer for *ALL* of His followers in John-seventeen, in verse-fourteen He stated: "I have given them Your Word; and the world has hated them, *BECAUSE* they are not of the world, even as I am not of the world." The devil persuades the lost to begrudge *ALL* those full of and walking in the *freedom-producing-Word-of-God;* because, born-again-Christians pose a threat to the-devil's-dark-dominion. *Satan pressures unsaved-people to pressure believers to STOP believing and preaching what Jesus COMMANDED US to believe and preach!* (Acts 4:18) The *TRUTH* (God's Word—John 17:17) exposes the devil's destructive-devices, and sets *FREE* his sin-slaves from his dominion. He is no longer their boss! (Romans 6:14) Therefore, to *gain* and *maintain* such CONTROL over the unsaved—*AND* through them to dominate the saved—Satan works on both sides of the equation. *On one hand, he hampers evangelical-efforts by harassing the evangelists, and on the other, he does everything he can to shield sin-slaves from their Gospel-message that makes repentant-sinners free.* (John 8:31-32) And,...

The Bible instructs believers to not be surprised at the negative-response from the world. First John 3:13: "Marvel not my brethren, if the world hates you." Peter also penned that: Sinners *"think it strange that you run not with them to the same excess of riot—speaking evil of you."* (1 Peter 4:3-5) Unbelievers believe that all who believe and practice the Gospel are weird. And, religion is plagued with the same foolishness. In Thessalonica, those unbelieving-Jews *RANTED* in raw-religious-rage: "Those who have turned this world upside-down have come here also." (Acts 17:6) The world with all its flaws seemed *OKAY* to those religious-leaders. *Paul and Silas were endeavoring to turn the world right-side-up again!* So, in reality, *it is unbelievers and religious-people who engage in really-weird-stuff!* (1 Corinthians 1:18-31, 2 Corinthians 10:12) They are blind to the truth that,...

God Himself will in the *NEAR-FUTURE* set all things *ARIGHT*, according to *HIS WORD. People who wait until that day to ARIGHT their selfish-attitudes and lifestyles will have waited too late. So, God urges sinners and all who trust in religious-doctrine instead of the blood shed by Jesus to repent now and call on the name of the Lord for their salvation!* Romans 10:9-13 tells them how.

Now that we have learned something about Satan's-evil-designs in this-evil-age, let us examine some of the sneaky-strategies pushing those devilish-designs. More Bright-Bible-Light on the way.

Chapter Six

Satan's-subtle-strategies

To be SUCCESSFUL in military-conquests, business-enterprises, political-campaigns, educational-projects or personal-endeavors, one must have a working-strategy. It works the same in the spirit-realm. The enemy of all mankind well-knows that essential-principle. Early on, the devil discovered that *the deception-strategy* worked for him *in persuading a number of other angels to rebel with him—then on the earth bringing about Adam's fall. Had the devil no ability to deceive other created beings, he would be unable to carry out his evil-designs.*

SELFISHNESS and DECEPTION work hand-in-glove. *A deceiver, motivated by selfish-ambition, uses deceit to selfishly-gain something belonging to another—or to rob another of something which was denied the deceiver. If plan A does not work, then plan B—If I cannot obtain it, then I will destroy it: If I cannot have it, neither can you!*

Selfish-folks seek only to satisfy their own interests; allowing no outside-interference with THEIR enjoyment. But, *demonically-motivated-people go beyond that, and satisfy their pleasures, not only with disregard for other people, but even at THE EXPENSE of other people! That is the-fallen-world-system-in-a-nutshell!* But now,...

Contrast such with God's command in Mark 12:31: "Love your neighbor *AS* you love yourself." *God did not forbid loving ourselves; but demanded that we believers treat other people like we desire to be treated.* Matthew 7:12 agrees. The system our Creator set up blesses all who cooperate with His system; *but disobedience reaps disaster without fail.* (Proverbs 10:29, Hosea 14:9)

Although people may be temporarily-advantaged by some of their selfish-deeds, *the devil is NEVER bettered by any of his cruelties.* With every temptation, the devil just stores up *MORE WRATH* for his own eternal-fiery-future. (Genesis 3:14-15, Isaiah 14:15, Romans 2:5)

DECEPTION is defined *AS* delusion, trickery, fraud, falsehood, hypocrisy, etc. To deceive one is to convince that one to accept *AS TRUE* what is in reality, *FALSE*—lying, cheating, leading into error—how Satan operates in this-fallen-world. Paul prophesied that at the end of this-evil-age *EVIL-PEOPLE WILL BECOME WORSE AND WORSE, DECEIVING and BEING DECEIVED* (2 Timothy 3:1-5, 13)—the Holy Spirit prophesying of every-sector-of-society, not only its-more-evil-sides. *Evil has existed on earth ever since the fall.* (Isaiah 10:1-2, Micah 2:1-2) So Paul had to mean that evil will *GREATLY-INCREASE* at the end of this-present-evil-age. Who could question that proven-prophecy? But, no matter Bible-Truth,...

Some church-members argue: "Such things happen out in the secular-world: Religion is different! The devil does not control the church as he does the world of the unsaved." *Such comments prove those people are either naive, or dishonest. The devil has done more damage to God's people through RELIGION than by all political and military-opponents put together in all of history. Religion is yet the devil's primary-weapon against God's church.* In addition to initiating pagan-religions (some of which persecute Christian-believers), *the devil has persuaded many church-leaders to reshape Christianity—reducing its saving-power and world-influence to near zero!*

False-belief-systems have to be the devil's idea. God would not form His own competition! Paul informed us in 1 Timothy 4:1: "In the latter-times, *SOME* Christians will *DEPART* from the faith [*so they must be IN the faith prior to departing FROM IT*] by giving heed to seducing-spirits, and doctrines-of-demons." Satan *USES* religion (including *altered-forms* of the Christian-faith) *to draw people away from Bible-Truth and Bible-Faith. Whether religious-people would agree, pulpits often become tools of the devil against God and True-Christianity!*

Roman-officials would not have crucified Jesus *had THE JEWISH-RELIGIOUS-LEADERS not demanded that He be crucified.* Those leaders had manipulated Rome's political-machine to accomplish their religious-agenda. *But Judaism itself becoming a hotbed-of-religious-and-political-instability*, Rome destroyed Jerusalem with its religious-sites in A.D. 70. After that the Roman-pagan-religions took up persecuting the Savior's church. The atrocities committed by the Roman-religious-adherents were much more severe, and lasted much longer, than did Jewish-persecution of Christians. Yet, in each case the devil used religious-zealots to attack God's church. If religion worked well for Satan back then, why would he abandon that *TOOL* now? (Acts 26:9-11) Enemies of the church are not just *OUT THERE SOMEWHERE!*

(My college-major was history; a significant-number of my degree-courses being *church-history*. Therefore, I have a solid-background in these historical-facts. And history-books, along with the internet, reporting 2000 years of church-history will substantiate my brief-and-general-statements along these historical-lines.)

Religious-friction abounds on our planet today; due to the many obvious-differences in doctrine among the myriad of religious-entities encircling the globe. *Gross-discrepancies plague the realm of RELIGION—with each system claiming to be THE BEST (some cases the ONLY)*

God-honoring way of life. Obviously, *they cannot all be propagating the TRUTH. The inconsistencies themselves ought to alert us that the religious-realm is deceiving us. Confusion is the order of the day.* But, from where does confusion come? *THE TRUE-GOD IS NOT THE AUTHOR OF CONFUSION!* (1 Corinthians 14:33) *THE DEVIL IS!* (James 3:14-16) And religion is one confusion-hot-spot in this world today! The devil has no greater-weapon.

Christianity is NOT a religion, but the Genuine-Faith; and so does not produce confusion. If there is only one True-Way, then there can be no confusion about which way is the Right-Way. Our only two choices are *life* and *death.* God's Word-Way assures life—death lies at the end of *ALL* other paths. (Deuteronomy 32:47, Proverbs 14:12, Matthew 7:13-14, John 14:6, Acts 4:12, Jude 3)

The Bible is the one and only Dependable-Source of truth about the *nature of God;* and the *origin, purpose,* and *destiny* of *men, angels* and *demons. God's Word is unique because of how it came about—being written by around* 40 *different authors from different-walks-of-life, and spanning over a-thousand-years. Only a handful of those human-Bible-writers were acquainted with any of the others, or lived during the SAME-time-period.* Those earlier-Bible-writers had no access to any later-works; yet, there exists a *glorious-consistency* among all of the different-Bible-Books. A truth that cannot be denied.

Moreover, *Holy Scripture has miraculously survived countless-onslaughts against its existence—attempts to distort its message, outlawing of every translation other than Latin, Hitler's book-burning-sessions, communist-atheism, and modern-textual-criticism.* Jesus told us in Luke 16:17 that *it is easier for this world to pass away than for Inspired-Scripture to become obsolete.* Not one word of God's promises to Israel failed! (1Kings 8:56)

THE PRECISE-FULFILLMENT of so many prophecies over hundreds of years, despite the overwhelming-odds against such, is proof the Bible is the only Word of God! One prophetic-detail has a 50/50 chance of fulfillment. It either WILL come to pass, or WILL NOT come to pass. Two prophetic-details increase those odds considerably. Dozens of prophetic-details increase the *ODDS* against them *ALL* being fulfilled almost to infinity!

Paul wrote in 2 Timothy 3:16 that *ALL* Scripture is God-breathed: Thus, *God recognizes as Scripture ONLY what the Holy Spirit moved men to write!* No document authored by human beings or initiated by demons is of God. *The devil is BEHIND ALL heathen-sacred-writings: The very reason he does not attack those writings as he does the Bible!* Gullible-souls fall for such falsehoods.

Moreover, whereas Holy Scripture does not hide the flaws of even its heroes, or condone their many errors, *heathen-religious-writings place all of their heroes on a pedestal untouchable by the common-man.* And as bait, some writings claim that their gods used to be humans who finally achieved godhood. Afterward, they revisited earth to offer their religious-advice to unfortunate-ones still imprisoned in the body. *MANY fall for those lies!*

Some pagan-writings establish the CASTE-SYSTEM; from which lower-class-victims have no hope of escape. Moreover, most promises of the pagan-religions apply to some future-existence—offering little or no improvement of present-circumstances! And not surprisingly,...

Distortions of Christianity push the SAME-SATANIC-LIE. Putting off most of the good-blessings until we get to heaven, we cannot determine which of the so-called-Christian-faiths is the *ONE*-genuine-faith. *Providing no real-here-and-now-standard, by which to evaluate their genuineness, that issue is reduced to mere-intellectual-academic-arguments. Real-Christianity is confirmed by the miraculous-power-of-God; when there is a real-need and where God finds someone who believes in and acts upon His promises to believers!* (Mark 6:5-6, 16:17-18, James 5:14-16) *GOD DOES NOT CHANGE, so NEITHER DO HIS COVENANT-PROMISES CHANGE!* (Malachi 3:6, Matthew 28:20, Hebrews 13:8) *God DEMANDS faith!*

So-called-DIFFERENT-Christian-faiths simply do not exist—from the True-Gospel-Perspective. Jesus warning that divided-kingdoms will *DISINTEGRATE*, why would He then proceed to divide His own Kingdom? (Matthew 12:25) Therefore, the devil has to be the spiritual-force behind *THE SPLINTERING OF THE MODERN-CHURCH*. No human-explanations for church-divisions make any sense; *in light of those Scripture passages that proclaim the existence of the ONE-faith and ONE-Body-of-Christ!* (1 Corinthians 12:12-13, Ephesians 4:4-6, Colossians 1:24, Jude 3) *Genuine-Christianity is the ONE-Body-of-Christ; consisting of genuine-Christians daily-practicing the ONE-genuine-faith!* (Matthew 7:21, 2 Timothy 2:19)

I have not yet pointed out the *UNFAIR-evaluation* of *WOMEN* in pagan-religious-writings. *They paint heaven as a man's-world; women to be SUBSERVIENT TO MEN in that realm, just as they are expected to be in this one.* Holy Scripture grants women a much-more-honorable-position, in both the-present-age and future-ages.

Now exposing the most-critical-discrepancy between the religious-junkyard of human-opinion and Holy Writ: The *unbridgeable-GAP* between the gods of the pagan-religions and the God of the *BIBLE*. In no writing of the world's-religions do we read about their gods coming to earth to *REDEEM MANKIND*. Some of them supposedly did return to the earth *to offer their advice. The Living-God, in contrast, offered Himself as a sacrifice in behalf of fallen-folks!* (Genesis 22:8, John 3:16, Acts 20:28) *The True-God BECAME A MAN, and took upon Himself mankind's sinfulness—in order to reconcile mankind to the Creator again!* (John 1:1, 14, 2 Corinthians 5:19)

To be saved, *Holy Scripture requires that we believe the good-news that Christ HAS ALREADY PURCHASED our complete-redemption by His own shed-blood.* (John 3:16, Acts 20:28, Romans 1:16, 8:32, 10:9-10, 1 John 3:20-22, 5:14-15) *And our redemption begins right now during this-lifetime* (2 Corinthians 6:2, 2 Peter 1:3-4); *then extends into all future-ages.* (Ephesians 2:7)

Why are there so many different-religions? *How can ALL of them be RIGHT? They all contradict one another in some way—and some fight against others.* Moreover, *honest-investigation reveals inconsistencies exist within each religion—even those so-called-Christian-religions!*

How does the devil get human beings to FALL for his lies? And why do human beings not use the intelligence God gave them? It matters not which lies the devil sells people on, *as long as the lies he sells them on prevents them from buying into the Gospel-Truth!* That is why he offers people so many *flavors* of religion. Having lots of choices tends to camouflage the real-issues; and keeps people in confusion and bondage—until it is too late.

Rejecting God's Word is the beginning of downward-progression toward destruction. John 10:10 tells us the devil comes to *steal,* to *kill,* and to *destroy.* Do you see the *downward-spiral?* Stolen goods can be returned or replaced. Bodily-death is more painful and detrimental than is material-loss; *yet some people have been raised from the dead.* But, destruction is the *FINAL-PAYMENT* of man's estrangement from God. Nobody escapes that monster, once it is initiated. (Isaiah 66:24, Mark 9:42-48, James 1:14-15, Revelation 14:10-11) Nevertheless, *those who have a WORKING-knowledge of God's Word, and act on that knowledge, overcome that evil-triplet by trusting God and obeying His Word NOW!* And yet,...

Satan robs immature-believers of their inheritance, by convincing them that: God having said one thing in His Word, *He really meant something entirely-different*: How the devil deceived Eve in Genesis 3:1-6! Similarly, the devil has talked most Christians into believing that God does things differently in these modern-days; *even though Scripture tells us plainly that God changes NOT.* Other gullible-souls are persuaded to trust ridiculous-falsehoods for their salvation rather than God's-plan of salvation through the shed-blood of Jesus Christ. Loss of material-goods disturbs one's peace (Satan stealing), whereas premature death curtails all opportunity to be a living-witness for Jesus on earth (Satan killing). But, being cast into that Lake of Fire is *IRREVERSIBLE* (the destruction-finale). Salvation *STOPS* downhill-slides!

John 12:40 states: "*HE* has blinded their eyes, and has hardened their heart; *SO THAT* they would not see with their eyes, or understand with their heart, and so be converted and *I* would *HEAL* them." First and third-persons dominate this verse, and I italicized *He* and *I*: "*He* has blinded them, lest *I* would *HEAL* them." If God was the *I*, Who wanted them healed, who was *he* who blinded them? *GOD IS NOT THE INITIAL-BLINDER!* The devil's kingdom is one of darkness! God is light! (John 8:12, Acts 26:16-18, James 1:16-17, 1 John 1:5-7). "The-god-of-this-world [Satan] has *BLINDED* the minds of those who believe not." (2 Corinthians 4:4)

The decision to *not believe* comes before the devil's-blinding commences. For, if the-devil's-blinding occurs first, he could prevent anyone he wants from accepting Christ. Such would put Satan in control of the destiny of every person on this planet. *No one could escape his dark-kingdom.* That cannot be. *The devil has never had such power! He cannot force his will upon free-wills!*

Based upon the Bible-Truth that Christ has already provided salvation for us means that our redemption is our decision. God awaits our free-will-choice to accept the salvation He offers. *Spurning Gospel-Truth sets that blinding into motion.* Matthew 13:15 states: "Their eyes *they* have closed; lest at any time, *they* would see with their eyes, and *I* would heal them." John 12:40 said *he* had blinded them. Matthew said God's own people had blinded themselves! Their cooperation with the enemy permitted him to *continue* that blinding-process; which hastened their destruction. However, if we have power to reject God's Word, *THEN* we can choose to believe it! (Incidentally, no one can *MAKE* such choice for anyone else. Each person has to make his or her own decision to believe or reject the Gospel-Message.) Thus,...

People *INITIATE* their own blindness. Then the devil furthers it. And, 2 Thessalonians 2:10-12 tells us that *God will then SEAL both their blindness and their doom.* Those who *REFUSE* salvation forfeit salvation: For, *God Himself will SEND strong-delusion on hardened-Christ-rejecters—so that they cannot believe and be saved.*

To *SPURN* the Gospel-message is to buddy-up with the devil; and *HELP* him achieve his dark-designs! For, *once the devil snares one victim, he works through that victim to begin the same process in the lives of others to make them victims.* Ephesians 2:2 says the devil is *that spirit, which now works in the sons-of-disobedience.* If people were not disobedient the devil could not work in or through them. Jesus said in Matthew 13:36-39 that evil-men are *SEEDS* the devil sows in the world, to lure other people into sin—and to harass all others who will not stoop to the devil's-level. *And there is no limit to the dirty-depths the devil will bring his victims down to!*

James 3:6 says that *the tongue of the lost-person, or the undisciplined-believer, is set on fire by Hell. Though the devil does not own or have any control over Hell, he plants every ugly, foul, corrupt and malicious-intent into the minds of deceived-people, so that they will gravitate toward that infernal-realm.* Satan *KNOWS* he is headed for that eternal-misery—and misery loves company!

Revelation 13:1-2 calls the devil the dragon, *which will someday invest in the Antichrist all of the ILLEGAL-AUTHORITY he has accumulated in this human-sphere through his deluded-followers.* By that time, *the church will have been removed from earth,* so almost everyone still left on earth will be Satan's deceived-pawns. Thus, the Antichrist will find it easy to persuade most of the ones *left behind* to perform nearly any deplorable-deed. However, the Antichrist will be stopped before all flesh is wiped out. (Matthew 24:22, Mark 13:20) And now,...

The following-three-chapters *explore that relatively-unexplored-biblical-territory that explains how everyone in the world—except those people who are born again—is connected to Adam—who by his sin joined himself to Satan—thereby connecting his unsaved-descendants to Satan. Only the new-birth breaks that evil-connection!*

Chapter Seven

The biblical-case—Acts 17:26

Was Adam the ancestor of all humankind? It might seem ridiculous to ask the question, because someone will likely comment: "Everybody knows that all human beings came from Adam!" What about those who push evolution? "But no Christian believes in evolution!" *The church-owned-and-operated-college I attended taught a Christianized-form of evolution!* Students were told that when humans evolved to Adam's stage of development, God put in them *a SOUL. So according to those church-college-professors, who were ALSO ordained-ministers, we must believe in evolution; even if the Bible has to be ALTERED to fit the evolution-theory.* That institution is an accredited-liberal-arts-college, *owned and operated by a church-denomination.* Although humanism wears many deceptive-faces, *the evolution-theory is the basic-teaching of ALL humanistic-thought—each one rejecting the biblical-account of creation in some way.* And sadly, *numerous-ecclesiastical-organizations incorporate some form of humanism into their doctrinal-systems—thereby embracing evolution.* Therefore, *you might be surprised at the number of people who claim to be Christians who question a vital-relationship between modern-man and the Adam of Eden! For, even many religious-folks,…*

Persuaded that modern-technological-breakthroughs will ENABLE modern-man to overcome past-limitations, and become better and better over time; THEREBY hold to the essential-tenets of that evolution-theory. Man, by the modern-god of scientific-research will solve all of his problems that are EVER-INCREASING in BOTH number and intensity. Those dreamers ignore this telling-truth:

Although science-labs have teemed with activity for centuries, *humanity faces more-and-greater-challenges today than at any other time in history!* Science cannot produce what we need most—life. *Spiritually-dead-men cannot produce life.* ONLY the Living-God—and nothing less than God—can give life! (John 10:10, Acts 17:28)

Denying a direct-link of modern-man to that original-ancestor—Adam—*the evolutionary-theory refutes God's Word—which clearly teaches that God created all living-things to reproduce after their own kind.* (Genesis 1:11, 21, 24-25, 28, 5:3) Evolutionists contend that man, by human-effort, is actually altering what he is—and thus improving his life. *Satan knows that if man attempts to solve his own problems, without reference to God, man will have no REAL-solutions.* (Psalms 46:1-2, 60:11-12, 121:2-8, 124:8, 146:3-4, Jeremiah 10:23, Acts 26:22, Philippians 3:3, Hebrews 4:16) Primary-Bible-proof,...

Acts 17:26 clearly says: *"God has made of one blood all nations of men to dwell on all the face of the earth." That establishes the connection of each human being to all others—regardless of geography, or time.* Only those who question God's Word will argue about it. It is true that certain Greek manuscripts do not have the word *blood*; but the truth is the same—*for even those Greek texts say that all nations came from ONE man. ADAM is the ancestor of all human beings—all colors included!*

Beside the Genesis-account of creatures reproducing after their own kind (including people) *and Acts 17:26, saying that every human being comes from ONE man—Adam; a third Scripture passage proves the same Bible-Truth; and totally-agrees with the other two.* Yet, it goes into even greater detail on the subject. Hebrews 7:4-14 *compares the high-priestly-ministries of JESUS CHRIST and MELCHIZEDEK.* Paul (For, *the Hebrews-letter must have been written by the apostle Paul—ONLY Paul had such revelation.*) emphasized that Abraham lived four-centuries before Moses' law was instituted. (Galatians 3:16-17) *Paul taught that because tithing was practiced long before Moses established that Levitical-priesthood, and tithing required a priest to receive tithes, there had to be a high priest back in Abraham's day.* Melchizedek was that priest. Moreover, Paul wrote that the pre-law-priest foreshadowed Christ; *Who receives tithes today; as Melchizedek and the Old-Covenant-priests did back in their times.* In that passage, Paul proved the oneness of the entire-human-race in that account of Abraham, his unborn-great-grand-son-Levi, and Melchizedek.

In verse nine, Paul wrote that *Levi figuratively paid tithes to Melchizedek* four-centuries *BEFORE* Levi was born! How did he pay tithes 400 years before his birth? "Levi also, who receives tithes, *PAID tithes IN Abraham.* For Levi was *IN THE LOINS* [the reproductive-organs] of his [great-grand-father-Abraham] that day Melchizedek met him [Abraham, with future-Levi in him]." Levi was born three-generations after Abraham's encounter with Melchizedek. This passage proves that *the human male holds in his body multiple-generations.* Hebrews 7:9-10 *proves that the SEEDS of all-future-generations existed in Adam's body.* If Abraham housed future-generations inside him, then Adam surely did! Have you heard that old-saying: *"You can count all of the seeds in an apple, but you cannot count all of the apples in a seed."? One apple-seed may potentially cover the entire* (habitable-) *earth with apple trees—every tree eventually producing MORE apples with MORE seeds.* The *SAME* was true of Adam—*because his Creator instructed him to reproduce his own kind—the very same as vegetables and critters.* (Genesis 1:26-28, 5:1-3) *APPLES produce APPLES—not some-other-kind-of-fruit. And humans produce humans; whose ancestry is traced back to Adam* (not monkeys)!

We are researching Bible-Truth about identification. All human beings are essentially identified with Adam, who first identified with God—made in His image—but later, through SIN, identified with the devil. (John 8:44) And since human beings—outside Christ—are related to Adam, who is identified with the devil, then ALL human beings who are NOT born again are identified—through the ADAM-CONNECTION—with the devil! Romans 5:12, 18-19: "By one man [Adam], sin entered the world, and *DEATH* [entered] by [Adam's] *SIN: So death has passed upon all men, because all have sinned.*" "By one offense [sin] of that *ONE MAN, ADAM, judgment came upon all men unto condemnation.*" "*By one man's disobedience, many* [ALL human beings] *were MADE to be SINNERS.*" One unwise-decision of Adam ALTERED both the nature and welfare of every creature on this planet—even flora and fauna. (Romans 8:19-23) And check this out,...

Romans 5:13-14: "*Death reigned* [over all creatures] *from Adam, unto Moses* [around 2000 years], *even over those who had not sinned after the similitude of Adam's* [one] *transgression.*" However: "Until the law sin was in the world: *But, sin is not imputed* [put to one's account] *when there is no law.*" Even though no one in following generations violated God's *direct-command* concerning the tree of knowledge of good and evil (*AS* Adam had), death continued to reign on the earth. Breaking Moses' law demanded the death-penalty! But, even before that law was instituted, death ruled throughout the human race. So, death is not linked to the direct-transgression of God's law: For even infants who have not committed any sin are liable to death. Thus, death is embedded in fallen-human-nature (for even babies have Adam's sin-nature). *Death is the result of WHAT A MAN IS, and not only WHAT HE DOES! People DO NOT BECOME sinners by sinning; but SIN BECAUSE THEY ARE SINNERS!*

Females do not determine the moral-constitution of their offspring. *THE MALES DO!* (Romans 5:12) *Adam's transgression transformed the reproductive-seeds in his body. AFTER HE BECAME A SINNER, HE COULD ONLY REPRODUCE SINNERS. And every generation of sinners produces the next generation of sinners.* Romans 3:23: "All [of Adam's descendants] have sinned, and thereby come short of the glory of God." *All unsaved-people are infected with Adam's sin-nature; carrying both spiritual and physical-death inside them.* "IN ADAM ALL DIE." (1 Corinthians 15:22) Romans 6:23 says plainly that "The wages of sin is death." Everybody (of-accountable-age) has sinned—because he or she descended from sinful-Adam. (Romans 5:12) Humanity is a fallen-race!

The apostle Paul endeavored to prove to the Jews of his day that they were just as guilty of *SIN* as were the Gentiles. Romans 3:9-10: "Are we [Jews] *BETTER* than they [those Gentile-sinners]? No, in no wise: For I have already proved [in Romans chapters-one and two] that both Jews and Gentiles are *ALL UNDER SIN*: Just as it is written: 'None is righteous [Jew nor Gentile], no, not one!'" *Those Jews had come to believe they were better than anyone else because they were the descendants of Abraham, and caretakers of Moses' law.* Paul reminded them that it was *OBEYING* the law (not possessing the law) that was pleasing to God; *and that they had come quite short of that required-and-expected-obedience!*

A large portion of New-Covenant-writings addressed the problem of *Gnosticism*—which asserted itself in the church's early-days. *Paul not only combated countless-Jewish-fables* (1 Timothy 4:7-8, 2 Timothy 4:3-4, Titus 1:14); *he found it necessary to put-the-brakes-on other heresies stemming from the Greek-culture. His epistle to those Ephesian-believers WARNED against establishing*

Gentile-practices in their congregation. (Ephesians 2:2, 11-13, 4:17-32) Paul's letter to Christians at Colossae, however, addressed problems, which already existed in that church-congregation. Colossians 2:8 and 18 prove that a false-teacher had sold those Christians on some doctrines that were *"after the tradition of men and after the rudiments of the world; and NOT after Christ." Paul told them that PHILOSOPHY and VAIN-DECEIT CHEAT.* (Colossians 2:8) Colossians 2:18 mentions the practice of worshipping angels—saying such practice *"beguiles* [deprives] us Christians of our [Godly-]reward." People do not come to Christ through some angelic-agency (*as taught by the Gnostics*), because the redemption Christ purchased for us by His own shed-blood is received by our trusting in Christ's-sacrifice; not angelic-activities.

John's epistles also dealt with *Gnosticism—a Greek-teaching that there exists a secret-source-of-knowledge, which only certain-enlightened-persons possessed.* And *ONLY* by that *special-knowledge* could one procure his or her salvation. *One had to be initiated into that inner-circle of those possessing that knowledge*—thus looking to people for one's salvation (according to that Gnostic-heresy). *The basic-lie of Gnosticism is that knowledge is superior to faith—which concept strikes at the HEART of the Gospel-message.* Another error is the superiority of spirit over flesh. Gnosticism contends that the spirit is the important part of people; whereas flesh is not even worth the bother. That heathen-concept split into *TWO* major branches—*one treading an ascetic-path, denying any comfort to the flesh; the other concluding that since the human body mattered not, its activities would be of little-consequence. Indulgence was the natural-result of that concept!* However, *as detrimental to individuals as was either of those Gnostic-doctrines, and practices, the EFFECT of such demonic-lies on the Gospel was worse:*

Denying the importance of the flesh downplayed the Bible-Truth that the Word of God was made flesh! How did John *COUNTER* those Gnostic-lies? *Inordinate-love for this world was forbidden.* (1 John 2:15-17) *And, the denial that God had been manifested in the flesh-realm was proven to be FALSE.* (1 John 1:1-3, 2:22-23, 4:1-6) Last, but not least, John destroyed that *KNOWLEDGE-HERESY.* (1 John 2:3-5, 19-21, 26-27, 4:5-6, 5:13, 20) Scripture clearly-declares that *faith in,* and *confession of,* Jesus Christ (Who *DID* come in the flesh to redeem mankind) is the only means of salvation; and *that faith comes by hearing the Word of God* (Divine-knowledge); *NOT* through some private-personal-knowledge; which only a few qualified-human-beings were able to impart. (John 14:6, Acts 4:12, Romans 10:9-10, 17, 2 Timothy 3:16, 2 Peter 1:20-21) *Doctrines that disparage flesh in our time descended from that Greek-Gnosticism!*

An unalterable-law throughout this universe is that no creature can transcend his or her present-status by his or her own-inherent-powers. *ONLY some being that is on a higher-plane-of-existence can LIFT us up to that higher-realm!* That destroys the evolution-theory. *Dead things cannot make themselves alive; nor can anything on a lower-plane lift itself to a higher-plane of existence!* Ephesians 2:11-12 also proves that we cannot advance ourselves by *OUR OWN* resources. Read this paragraph over and over again, to assimilate that Bible-Truth into your consciousness! *Creatures are not creators.* We are dependent on God for both existence and promotion!

Despite our modern-technological-advances, *human nature almost always takes the low-road. And even the current-knowledge-explosion exists only because of the prophecy God gave Daniel!* (Daniel 12:4) *Human beings did not CREATE modern-technical-knowledge; they only discovered it.* And, those scientific-breakthroughs have become possible for us human beings to discover, only because the Creator created the principles-of-physics; *and then prophesied through Daniel that they would be discovered in the last days! It should be obvious that,...*

Denial of the *NEED* for redemption does not remove the *NEED*. Therefore, feeble-human-attempts to render God obsolete (despite God being the only One Who can truly help us) is utter-foolishness. *Mankind's only hope is to openly acknowledge its dire-predicament, and then believe for and receive the only redemption available to the human race—Jesus Christ.* (Acts 4:10-12) It is not a failure to admit that one is a member of Adam's fallen-race—because Christ came to save Adam's fallen-race! (Luke 19:10) Moreover, upon receiving redemption, *one does not remain Adam's-sinful-kin—but enters a whole-new-existence within.* Because,...

When one under Holy-Spirit-conviction repents and accepts God's plan of salvation (by believing in Christ's blood, shed in behalf of truly-repentant-ones) a miracle occurs in that individual. *His or her old-sinful-self dies, and a new-righteous-self takes its place.* (2 Corinthians 5:17-21) Plus, one's ties to sinful-Adam being severed, all bondages to Satan are broken as well; *and the new-creature is united to God; the SOURCE of abundant-life.* (John 5:24-26) An unbeatable-salvation-plan! It would be most unwise to reject it. Further-proof of that-truth:

Chapter Eight

Historical-evidence of the fall

Abruptly, *Adam's sin-nature manifested itself in the first of his progeny.* In jealous-rage, Cain murdered his younger brother Abel. (Genesis 4:1-15) Jesus said that Satan was a murderer from the beginning of his career as Satan (John 8:44), and Adam had been envenomed by the same degenerate-nature. *So the seed-producing-after-its-kind-principle, having been activated in Adam, it was only a matter of time before such evil-inclinations surfaced in one, or more, of Adam's family-members.* Of course, the devil cannot manipulate people like robots; or else he could have incited both sons to rebel against their parents; or, tempted Cain to murder Abel sooner. *The devil has to convince his unsuspecting-victims that another human being has victimized them—so that they feel justified in attacking that other human being.* Even though God had warned Cain about *SIN'S-BID* for him (Genesis 4:6-7), the man failed to heed the admonition. *Cain permitted temptation to overcome him—convincing himself that his brother Abel, RATHER THAN HIMSELF, was the reason God had disapproved his offering.*

Satan strives to keep people IGNORANT of the reality that he is somehow connected to all of their problems! If they knew the devil was the *spiritual-force* behind their woes, they would resist the devil *BEFORE* dealing with people. Of course, *human beings ARE involved in many of our circumstances*: But according to Ephesians 6:12, *the devil and fallen-angels, working in the atmospheric-realm, are the ultimate-forces behind ALL our problems. Every human-predicament has SPIRITUAL-ROOTS!*

Abel's personality was *OPPOSITE* Cain's—giving the devil opportunity *TO CAUSE FRICTION* between them. The Greek *diabolos* (devil) signifies: *A being that forces either itself or something else between two personalities for the purpose of separating the two*—slanderer. *Satan attempts to block relationships—or to inflict irreparable-damage upon relationships between people and people, and between people and their Creator and Redeemer.*

The spiritual-*ENEMY* of the human race specializes in fomenting jealousy between members of households and churches. Many cases exist of siblings engaging in vicious-legal-battles over family-inheritances. Even the Bible records many examples of family-strife: The devil provoked *ferocious-conflicts* between Jacob and Esau, Joseph and his brothers, King David's quarreling-sons, and infamous kings of Israel's later-history; *whose first ACT after their coronation was to murder their brothers; lest one of them lay claim to the throne.* (Genesis 27:41, Judges 9:1-6, 2 Samuel 13:1-33, etc.) In addition,...

Destroying marriages is one more specialty of Satan. In the setting where love and kindness *OUGHT* to rule, hate, violence and even murder often occur. First Peter 3:7 explains why Satan wants to cause *friction* between marriage-partners—especially among Christians: *Strife impedes unity and hinders prayer.* Remember, the Lord promised that *if any two believers on earth would be in agreement regarding any petition to God, heaven would honor their prayer.* (Matthew 18:19) Psalms 133 *agrees that blessing and anointing abide where brethren dwell together in unity.* So, *it should be obvious why the devil ASSAILS every form of God-ordained-unity among men.* Disunity *OPENS A DOOR* to the devil to disrupt human activities, and gives him a strategic-advantage over the *OUTCOME* of disjointed-human-endeavors.

What is even worse, that same devilish-mindset has also invaded the church. The *SAD*-fact that the Body of Christ, which our Lord established in unity, has since divided itself into *numerous-opposing-denominations* is a major result of Satan's anti-God activities. In Christ's final-prayer-request before the cross, *He petitioned His Heavenly Father to provide perfect, peaceful, perpetual-UNITY among ALL the members of His CHURCH* (John 17:20-23)—*and there is not a hint to be found in all the New Testament that He ever rescinded that request!* In addition, *Paul and other writers warned of the dangers of church-division.* (Romans 12:16, 15:5-6, 16:17-18, 1 Corinthians 1:10-13, 3:3, Ephesians 4:4-6, Philippians 1:27, 2:2, 4:2, 1 Peter 3:8, Jude 3) Understand this,...

The very definition of denomination denotes division: To differentiate between entities—assigning to each one A DIVERGENT-IDENTITY. Such works well in finances: It is convenient to have one, five, ten, twenty, fifty and one-hundred-dollar-bills—*MONEY*-denominations. It is advantageous to be able to recognize the *differences in quantity* among those federal-reserve-notes, in order to avoid getting *RIPPED OFF* in business-deals. However, when it comes to the church, the Savior authorized *NO* division, in either quantity or quality. *The splintering of the church,* then, *lies upon the shoulders of its human-leadership—and it is definitely ripping people off! Since denominationalism hides from Christians the truth that there is ONLY ONE Body of Christ, the devil must be the fomenter of the freakish-fracturing of today's church! No religious-argument can successfully indict the Godhead for it!* And, the devil's *PURPOSE* for those divisions is to standardize internal-disunity and powerlessness.

For close to 2000 years, *many ecclesiastical-leaders have systematically-persecuted and exterminated their religious-enemies, in order to maintain the status-quo of their ecclesiastical-organizations.* Such cannot be God's will—for murder is the devil's nature and purpose. *"No murderer has eternal-life abiding in him."* (1 John 3:15) Church-members engaging in murder cannot possibly belong to the real-Body-of-Christ! They not possessing eternal-life, they must be the *false-brethren* Paul spoke of in 2 Corinthians 11:26 and Galatians 2:4. *Contrary to certain-religious-beliefs, heavenly-approval does NOT grace every religious-institution!* God regards only those who are *WASHED* in the shed-blood of the Lamb; *AND* whose lifestyle reflects that *INNER*-transformation.

Reading some portions of the Bible, especially in the more-modern-versions, reminds us of news-broadcasts today—with the disgusting-news beginning in Genesis. *The hostility Cain expressed toward Abel is a portrait of modern-sinful-human-nature—murder being common in the media-headlines—Adam's sinful-nature manifesting in society today; as in ancient-times—and getting worse by the day, as the Bible prophesied!* (2 Timothy 3:1-5)

The almost *unimaginable-perversions* and *shocking-atrocities* committed more often and by more and more people today are not just weird-accidents-of-nature, or the fruit-of-chance. They have been planned by Satan, and committed by deceived-people—whose history can be traced back to Eden's-original-sinners. If lost people today are not linked to *sinful-Adam*, what may explain those unmistakable-similarities? *Modern-man is sinful-Adam multiplied many times over—both in number and defilement—Bible-Truth fulfilled in modern-times!*

Scripture portrays human-nature *JUST as it is*; and *does not excuse man's aberrant-behavior, nor champion weird-lifestyles like fake-news-media generally do.* The fallen-world-system is attempting to pressure everyone to accept man's ugly-side as normal; whereas the Bible reveals a *definite-difference* between what is acceptable to God and what is not! Our Savior never compromises His Godly-character, nor alters His eternal-commands; *while Satan's crowd pushes people to become more and more unconventional as time goes on*—proving the devil is a heavy-influencer of most-modern-media. However, *people who question God's Word are the unreliable and unprofitable-witnesses!* Jeremiah 8:9 proves that.

The Bible reveals how the devil initiates a distorted-mindset or condition in one person, *and then uses him or her to transplant the SAME-ABNORMALITY in others; like a filthy-hog smearing filth on everything it touches.* Today, we are surrounded by filthy-hogs (so to speak) on every side—thanks to the *filthy-news-media, filthy-college-and-university-professors, filthy-tech-company-ceos*, and more and more *filthy-federal-state-and-local-government-officials*. We find in 2 Corinthians 4:4 that the *"god-of-this-age"* (*SATAN*) *blinds people who believe not*; and Matthew 15:14 tells about *the spiritually-blind attempting to lead other blind-folks*. Neither can see the pitfalls in the road ahead; *and Jesus said that both will sooner or later fall into the ditch*. The devil wants people to fall and get hurt, and he uses those he has deceived already to do the hurting. Blind-leaders not only injure themselves; *they influence other gullible-souls to do the same*. Satan's fools and tools—including preachers!

Think about the *EASE* of spreading *DISEASE*. *Once one person becomes infected, that person can endanger an entire-community with sickness or death*. The *SAME* is true of sin and perversion. Many may never face the Adversary personally (After all, the devil may be in only one place at a time—with the planet's population being about 8,000,000,000.). So, he only need send someone our way whom he has already contaminated with some perversion to begin the same-process in us. (Galatians 5:7-10) Paul said leaven spreads throughout an entire-lump-of-dough, in which it is mixed. He explained that *a divisive-man who was leaven in a spiritual-sense had polluted some Christians in those Galatian-churches.* In that same passage, Paul said that the human-polluter would face God's judgment for leading believers astray. *Preventing pollution in one's life and ministry is always less-messy than cleaning up the mess afterwards!*

Scripture shoots-straight, whereas the *FAKE*-media distort the facts in almost every case. *Scripture exposes the real-culprit behind all human woes, while the world points fingers at scapegoat-personalities it wants out of the way.* The Roman emperor Nero accused *Christians* of burning Rome, and Adolf Hitler blamed the *Jews* for Germany's bankrupt-economy in World War II. Adam's descendants have a tendency to blame other people for their woes—*as evidenced by civil-lawsuits skyrocketing today. Few are willing to acknowledge personal-guilt in what are often self-imposed-tragedies.* Blinding oneself to ones's own guilt, however, does not shield one from the consequences of one's own guilt! (Galatians 6:7-8)

What about sickness and disease? Is illness a mere freak-of-nature? Or, ought we all (*including Christians*) *EXPECT* to suffer sickness from time to time? *Sickness is NOT NORMAL; at least from God's-perspective. Satan and sin are behind ALL abnormalities!* Neither sickness nor disease existed on this earth before Adam and Eve transgressed. And just as sin spreads from one person to another, so does disease. Although most everyone is aware of that truth, many people (*including preachers*) are confused regarding the *source of illness. And some theologians even claim that sickness is a blessing-from-on-high.* THAT IS ONE BIG LIE! Just as sin is a product of Adam's fallen-nature, springing from his union with Satan, *SO ARE sin's-consequences—sickness and pain, poverty and lack, defeat and death.* God's Word always LINKS sickness with the devil—*and not one Bible-verse teaches that sickness is a blessing-in-disguise from our Loving Heavenly Father to His faithful-followers!!!*

Deuteronomy 28:1-14 is a list of covenant-blessings *Old-Covenant-patrons experienced by their obedience to those covenant-demands—and sickness appears not on that blessing-list.* But, the remaining 54 verses in that chapter lists every kind of disease and bodily-infirmity; *calling them all CURSES—and good-health is not on the CURSE-LIST.* Also, Exodus 15:26, 23:25, Deuteronomy 7:15, Job 2:7, 42:10, Psalms 103:5, 107:20, Proverbs 4:20-22, Isaiah 53:4, 10, Jeremiah 17:14, Hosea 11:3, Matthew 4:23-24, 8:16-17, 9:35-10:1, Luke 13:11-16, Acts 10:38, 1 Corinthians 12:4-11, 28, James 5:14-15, 1 Peter 2:24 and 3 John 2 prove that *BODILY-HEALTH* is *GOD'S-WILL* for His faithful-people. No exceptions!

Being blind to biblical-truth is the first step toward eventual-destruction; for it sets one up for *entrapment.* "Those who have been *ensnared* by the devil are *taken captive* by him to do his will." (2 Timothy 2:26) And the only way to escape those traps is to repent and accept Divine-deliverance. *The devil entraps people, in order to gain and maintain control over them, and then use them to entrap other people!* Second Peter 2:19: "*While they* [the ensnared-ones] *promise them* [prospective-victims] *liberty, they themselves ARE SERVANTS of corruption." The lost do not realize the evil-disposition they inherited from Adam—and they will never know, unless someone tells them about their sinfulness; AND that Jesus Christ bore the punishment for the sins of all those who repent and believe the Gospel.* (John 3:16, Romans 10:9-10)

Satan is a fierce-taskmaster to all under his power. The *ONLY* people who can put Satan to flight are those genuine-Christians, who know that they can, and who know how to use the name of Jesus against him—and who daily walk in the reality of the New Covenant. Acts 19:11-20 tells of seven non-Christian-Jewish-exorcists who attempted to use the name of our Lord to deliver a demon-possessed-man without personally knowing the "Jesus whom Paul preached." The men were powerless before the supernatural-power of that possessed-man. The evil-spirit in the man said: *"Jesus I know and Paul I know; but who are you?"* They *TRIED* to get the *SAME* results Paul did, using Jesus' name as a magic-charm. No Satan-victim can cast demons out of other victims!

The devil uses empty-promises which sound good to LURE people into doing evil; or uses fear and threats of personal-harm to PRESSURE his sin-slaves to do HARM to others. Those ensnared by Satan are unable to sleep unless they harm somebody else. (Proverbs 4:16) Fear has torment. (1 John 4:18) So if the devil can keep one in fear, he can control that one through that fake-fear. *It matters not if the fear-phantoms ever materialize; the torment of inner-trepidation makes the fearer miserable.* (Proverbs 12:25, 15:15) Anxiety muddles the mind and produces confusion and distorted-perspectives of both people and events—the devil's delight. *Envy, strife and confusion are of the devil, and work evil in ill-informed-Christians, as well as in the unsaved.* (James 3:14-16)

The next chapter scripturally and historically-reveals just how low the devil wants to take, and does take, the fallen-human-race today. The unquestioned-accuracy of Bible-prophecy is proven by news-coverage every day.

Chapter Nine

Human-hopelessness

After the previous-chapter, some readers just might be inclined to believe human-life is no longer worth the living—*concluding that there is NO HOPE for mankind.* That is actually one of the responses I want to achieve in the minds and hearts of everybody poring over these pages. *Mankind ON ITS OWN has NO HOPE of survival!* (Ephesians 2:12) However, the Creator did not leave us with no way out. *He has provided the human race with a solution to its hopelessness. But we must first confess that WITHOUT GOD we are hopeless!* (Ephesians 2:12) Those thinking that their Godless-lifestyle needs only a *surface-touch-up* do not realize the trouble they are in. The Lord even commanded *ALL* of the Jews to repent—*do a one-hundred-eighty-degree-about-face.* Of course, they perceived nothing amiss regarding their lifestyles; so in self-defense, they accused the Savior of being out of touch with reality. (Mark 3:21, John 8:48) Salvation is *NOT AN ADD-ON* to one's current-sinful-lifestyle; but rather, *is an EXCHANGE of one's current-sinful-lifestyle for the new-creation in Christ; whereby the old-things of a sinner's sinful-lifestyle are terminated, and all things become NEW in Christ!* (2 Corinthians 5:17-21)

Most first-century-Jews LINKED all of their problems to Roman-occupation of Judea. Jewish-religious-leaders labored to keep their Roman-conquerors pacified. (John 11:48) *Those Jews blamed an entity outside themselves as the source of their problems; not realizing, or at least not being willing to admit, that their undesirable-living-conditions had come about as much by their own-fallen-*

nature as by that outside-entity. (John 8:34-36) Christ urged the Jews to trade their old-way-of-life for Divine-life; explaining in Luke 17:33: "Whoever wants to *save* his life [just as it is] will lose it; and whoever *loses* his life [for being faithful to God] will *preserve* it." The Lord told Nicodemus in John 3:3 that people must be born again (from above) to enter the Kingdom of heaven. *NO* exceptions! *So people who do not get born again before they die will FACE eternal-destruction.* (Matthew 23:15, John 3:18-21, 36, 8:24) *The Jews thought some people experienced super-tragic-deaths for being exceptionally-evil.* But, Jesus made it clear that: "Unless you repent, you will all likewise perish." (Luke 13:1-5) Yet,...

Many insist that man is not evil by nature; *but that his problems stem from the flawed-environment instead of from that moral-flaw lodged within the human-spirit.* Well, who flawed the environment? *God made the earth and everything in it. BUT* it was Adam's union with the devil, which introduced the curse on earth—*and every cursed-generation* (of both humans and animals) *since has suffered the cursed-consequences!* (Colossians 2:8, 1 Peter 1:18-19) Humankind is on a downward-spiral, descending at an accelerating-pace. (2 Timothy 3:13)

The world's *actual-condition* is revealed only in Holy Scripture—*the only source of information that honestly describes the pitiful-condition of the fallen-human-race!* "*ALL NATIONS* before God *are as nothing*; and *counted by Him less than nothing and worthless.*" (Isaiah 40:17) Yet, people see themselves as significant, *even without* the Creator, Sustainer, and Redeemer. Human-pride is *exaggerated-self-esteem—false-estimation of one's own worth, independent of God!* There being no real-reason for human-haughtiness, it dares to flaunt itself against God everywhere one turns in today's twisted-world.

Identity-Crisis —— Cause and cure

Adam having become *intricately-connected* to Satan through sin, each generation (to the present) shares in that *SAME unnatural-union* through *natural-childbirth*. And because of that unfortunate-union, humankind is sinking to lower and lower moral-depths. It began right after Adam was expelled from the Garden of Eden; and is fully-described in Romans 1:19-32: "What might be known about God is manifest in them [all humans]; *for God HAS SHOWN IT TO THEM*. For the invisible-things of God from the creation of this world are clearly-seen; they being understood by the things that were created; even His eternal-power and Godhead—so that they are *WITHOUT EXCUSE*: Because, although [from the start, all human beings] knew God, they glorified Him not as God, neither were they thankful, but [instead], became *VAIN* in their imaginations; and their foolish-heart was darkened. Thus, professing themselves to be wise, they became fools—changing the glory of the incorruptible-God into images like corruptible-human beings, birds, and animals; and even creeping-things. Therefore, God also gave them up to uncleanness through the lusts of their own hearts; to dishonor their own bodies between themselves: *Who changed the TRUTH of God into a LIE*, and worshipped and served the creature more than the Creator; the One Who is blessed forever. For this cause God gave them up to *VILE-AFFECTIONS*—For, even the women changed their natural-[sexual-]use into what is against nature—Likewise men, leaving the natural-use of the woman [*in marital-sexual-intercourse*], burned in their lust toward one another—men with men working what is shameful; and receiving within themselves the consequences of their [moral-]error; which was proper. Moreover, since they did not like to retain God in their knowledge, God turned them over to a reprobate-mind, to do things not fitting [*into His plan for creation*]: They now being filled with *ALL* unrighteousness, fornication, wickedness, covetousness, maliciousness; being full of envy, murder, debate, deceit, malignity: [They became] whisperers, backbiters; even haters of God, despiteful, proud, boasters, inventors of evil things, disobedient to parents; having no understanding, covenant-breakers, without *ANY* natural-affection, implacable, unmerciful: Who, [though] knowing the judgment of God, that they who commit such things are worthy of death, *not only do the same, but have pleasure in others who do them!"*

But, *as bad as were human-rebels at the very start of this-evil-age,* Paul prophesied in 2 Timothy 3:13 that *as time goes on evil-men will become worse and worse; deceiving and being deceived.* And, that is exactly what is going on around the globe—the increase accelerating over the past-decade with great speed! The result,...

A gigantic-gamut of putrid-perversions is pervading the feeble-fabric of pitiful-progressive-political-policies. *And none of those perversions make any sense to sane-minds*: A sure-sign they are the devil's-designs. A sure-sign, as well, that the devil's time to run loose on earth is fast coming to a close. He is pulling out all the stops *TODAY* in his bid to destroy everything he can destroy, while he still walks around seeking someone to devour. (1 Peter 5:8) Satan uses perversion-deceptions to push people to destroy themselves. For example,...

In Romans-one, the primary-perversions had to do with *sexual-deviation* and *reorientation—each designed by the devil to thwart God's plan for creation; especially the human-portion of it.* However, today, not only same-sex-marriage (of which there is no such thing) are they pushing, *but extending those perversions to the sexual-exploitation of minors—making such perversion lawful—with the only consent required being of the exploiters!!!*

And, not only mis-matching sexual-partners, which God does not approve—*but even trying to alter the very gender of the victims of this modern-madness—trying to turn boys into girls, and girls into boys—even preschool-children! And, making it unlawful for anybody to inform the parents about such operations on their kids!!!*

GENDER CANNOT ACTUALLY BE ALTERED! THUS, THE VICTIMS BODIES ARE JUST MUTILATED. The devil wants the bodies, souls and spirits of all human beings to be mutilated beyond recognition. So the devil must be behind the medical-mutilation of kids. Whereas Wokists insist that there are many genders, even animals know there are only TWO GENDERS—male and female. Thus, even animals are smarter than those pitiful-perverts.

The devil is out to steal, kill and destroy all creation; (John 10:10) *especially the human-portion of it. And the senseless-mutilation of human bodies is only one of the devil's evil-maneuvers in achieving that evil-agenda. By distorting human bodies, the devil achieves several-evil-results. One: TO CLUTTER OUR IDENTITY. Another: TO DESTROY OUR DIGNITY. Finally: TO MAKE SURE OUR DESTINY IS HELL* (This book-sub-title!) *If people know not who or what they are (their actual-IDENTITY), they will likely have little or no concern over their DIGNITY, or their DESTINY—so will make little or no preparation to secure their eternal-well-being. The devil's delight!*

If BOTH the IDENTITY and DIGNITY of the individual is in DISARRAY, family-structure becomes obsolete; and human-government is demeaned because all integrity is gone. More and more people will come to the conclusion that life is not worth the living—increasing suicides—as is the case nation-wide and world-wide—one more part of the devil's over-all-plan to steal, kill and destroy.

Another obvious result of all this is that the nations will be weakened—Satan's-original-plan. (Isaiah 14:12) Social-weakness leads to national-weakness—and that is spreading across the globe. Moreover, such madness is not confined to sinners—but is in the church too!

Galatians 4:8-9: "*WHEN YOU* [as unsaved-Gentiles] knew not God, you did service to beings that by nature are not gods [but are demons]. But now, after you have known God, or rather are known of God, *how turn you back AGAIN to the WEAK and beggarly-elements* [of the world]; whereunto you desire to be in bondage?" "*That which is highly-esteemed among men is abomination* in the sight of God.*" (Luke 16:15) *God scrapped the world-system of Noah's-day; and is about to do it again!*

James also said: "Know you not that the friendship of the world is enmity with God? Whosoever, therefore, will be a friend of the world[-system] is the very enemy of God!" (James 4:4) If language means anything, that is God's denunciation of the present-world-system. He instructs His people to have nothing to do with it. *The world-system ENGENDERS bondage.* (Galatians 4:3)

Three elements of this world-system are: "The *LUST* of the flesh, the *LUST* of the eyes, and the *PRIDE* of [a degenerate-]life[style]." (1 John 2:15-17) To buddy-up with this world-system is to side with God's enemy; for no man can serve two masters! (Matthew 6:24)

We were all born into the world ALREADY separated from God through that sin-nature we inherited from our earth-parents—who inherited their sin-nature from their earth-parents—all the way back to Adam and Eve. And although a Christian-family-atmosphere does enhance a child's spiritual-understanding, helping it make right choices in life, the final decision to accept God's way or reject it lies with each individual child; *as it reaches its own-particular-age-of-accountability. (The age at which different children become accountable to God varies; no two are the same.)* Since God granted to every human being a free will, each has to decide whether to remain in an *inherited-state-of-opposition-to-God,* or to repent, and accept the Gospel-Truth about receiving salvation. (However, the blood of Christ covers children until they reach the age-of-accountability and begin their own life of sin. Read Matthew 19:13-14, Mark 10:13-15, Luke 18:15-17 and Romans 7:9-11.) Also, realize this,...

The new-birth does not reverse the nature of man's flesh. *That mortal* (death-doomed-)*body* (Hebrews 9:27) *will not become immortal until the rapture of the church.* The believer's body, however, has been redeemed from all the curses which affect the body—even now in this-evil-age. (Galatians 3:13) The Greek word *redeemed* in that verse means *to buy up all there is to buy.* That is a commercial-term; not the same one used to signify our final-redemption. Through the recreated-spirit, *Divine-Life is released into the believer's natural-body, to fill it with health and wholeness!* (Proverbs 4:20-24, Romans 8:11, 2 Corinthians 4:10) However, *that blood-bought-blessing only produces HEALTH in the body: It does not alter the mortal-nature of the body.* Even Christians die physically. *The believer's spiritual-rebirth does not alter the reproductive-seeds in the believer's body. Spiritual-children are not brought forth by natural-conception.* As sweet as little ones are when they arrive on this planet, they do have Adam's-fallen-nature, and will eventually need to be *BORN AGAIN. It takes spiritual-seeds* (of the Gospel-message) *to produce spiritual-rebirths!*

Spiritual-death is separation from God—the Source of *LIFE*—and union with the devil, the lord of *DEATH*— *who can produce nothing but death!* (John 8:44, 10:10)

That condition of being separated from God may be remedied during this-age by the unsaved-person being born again. *But, if the person continues to be separated from God their entire-lifetime on earth, and does not get born again, the unsaved-person will be separated from God throughout eternity in "the Lake of Fire prepared for the devil and his angels."* (Matthew 25:41) The Lake of Fire was prepared for the devil and all other rebellious-angels—*NOT* for humanity. Also notice that the Lake of Fire was *prepared; not created—which means that God prepared it AFTER the original-creation.* Notice too that it was prepared for the *DEVIL,* and not for Lucifer. God did not create Lucifer *EVIL,* but perfect. (Ezekiel 28:15) It was only *after* Lucifer rebelled against God that God *PREPARED* that place of torment *FOR* the devil and his fallen-angelic-followers. Since the Lake of Fire was not part of the original-creation, *that degrading-destination was surely not God's plan for any of His creatures!* Yet, Jesus taught that *rebellious-people* too will be confined to that infernal-region; just like the devil, demons, and angels which *ABANDONED THEIR FIRST HABITATION.* (Matthew 8:28-29, 25:41, 2 Peter 2:4, Jude 6)

Neither Satan, other fallen-angels, nor demons, can get reconciled to God. *Their eternal-destiny was sealed the very day they rebelled* (in the blazing light of Truth) *against the Creator.* There existed no tempter to tempt Lucifer; and *NO EVIL* already existed in God's universe. Thus, there is *NO* redemption for *ANY* of them! (Isaiah 14:15, Ezekiel 28:15) Having *NO HOPE* of redemption, Satan has no personal-restraint against harming other creatures. He is, therefore, no-kind-personality! Yet,...

We human beings *CAN* receive that salvation Christ provided for us on the cross. So, the human race is not really hopeless after all! The Bible says that Jesus took upon Himself the nature of man, not angels. (Hebrews 2:16) That passage is definite proof that angels cannot possibly partake of New-Testament-redemption. *Angels consist not of flesh and blood, as human beings do; and the Lord's sacrifice was made in behalf of the creatures, in whose form He came!* (Romans 8:3, Philippians 2:7) However, *salvation may be received only by those who believe, and acknowledge, that Christ was CRUCIFIED IN THEIR BEHALF and WAS RAISED FROM THE DEAD, and thus has become THEIR OWN PERSONAL SAVIOR.* (Acts 4:12, Romans 10:9-10, 1 Timothy 4:10)

Colossians 1:21 is another testimony of God's-view of the *UNSAVED*: "*You* [Gentiles-now-Christians], *were* [in the past] *alienated* [from God]; *being His enemies in your minds by your wicked-works.*" Being in union with God's enemy, lost-man is separated from his Creator— and is God's adversary, like the devil! Ephesians 2:12: "*At that time you were without Christ, being aliens from the citizenship of Israel, strangers from the covenants of promise, and having NO HOPE, and without God in this world.*" This world being without God means this world is without hope—as far as its ability to save itself. But, *God provided salvation for the hopeless through Christ!*

The cross is heaven's equalizer! No one can bypass the cross and be saved. But, anyone and everyone may be saved by accepting what Christ did on that cross in their behalf. And God put that salvation-information in the Bible, and sends missionaries around the planet to get that good-news to everybody living on it. (Matthew 28:18-20, Mark 16:15-20, John 20:21, Acts 1:8) *New Testament believers have an age-long-commission*: For, *we are commanded to preach the Gospel of salvation to the ends of the earth, right up to the end of this present-age.* Whoever believes that will be saved. (John 3:16)

Emphasizing once again—*Our Savior has ALREADY purchased our salvation! By His death on the cross, He achieved our freedom from the devil, sin, and all of sin's curses!* (John 3:16, Romans 6:23, Galatians 3:13-14, 1 Corinthians 6:20, Colossians 1:13, Titus 3:4-5, James 1:18, Revelation 1:5-6) But, individuals are responsible for *receiving* that salvation. *It is not the responsibility of the Savior Who provided salvation! And salvation has to be received GOD'S-WAY—by one's personal-faith.* (Acts 2:38, 3:19, 4:12, Romans 10:9, Titus 3:5, 1 Peter 1:23) Thus, people who decline Divine-redemption, or refuse to gain it God's-way, *deprive themselves of redemption.* (Hebrews 10:26-31) And God Himself actually becomes their enemy! (John 3:18, 36, 2 Thessalonians 1:8-9)

I have purposefully-presented this positive-portion of pertinent-passages to persuade perusers to perceive my pivotal-points. Yet I have a whole-heap of heaven's-highlights to hopefully-help hurting-humanity lay hold of heaven's-*HIGHWAY—THE WRITTEN WORD OF GOD! See what God says about the right way and wrong way in these pivotal-passages*: Isaiah 35:8-10, 40:3, John 10:9, 14:4-6, Acts 9:2, 18:24-26, 19:9, 23, 22:4, 24:14, 22, Hebrews 10:20, 2 Peter 2:2, 15, 21.

The preceding-revelation has LAID the foundation for an understanding of the succeeding-portion of this book about the price Jesus Christ had to pay to purchase our salvation—and about the salvation He purchased. After reading and heeding this unique-revelation, you will not view your redemption the same ever again.

Chapter Ten

Hefty-price-tag—Hebrews 2:14

Only after comprehending the utter-hopelessness of the inhabitants of the *lost-world* may we begin to grasp the depth of our-Savior's-*SACRIFICE* for mankind. For, *those who believe human beings have an innate-ability TO RESCUE THEMSELVES from their problems despise any sort of Divine-intervention in their lives. Even many believers do not want to believe that on the cross Christ was DEFILED WITH THEIR SINS, THEIR SICKNESSES, THEIR CURSES, THEIR POVERTY, THEIR SEPARATION FROM GOD, THEIR TORMENT IN HADES—preferring to SEE their Lord as a nice-and-lovely-Savior—Who would not DIVULGE their corrupt and hypocritical-personality. They cannot envision Christ becoming filthy with THEIR FILTH! But, CHRIST SUFFERED NOT FOR ANY SIN OF HIS OWN.* Like it or not, *ALL THAT HE BORE ON THAT CROSS HAD YOUR AND MY NAMES STAMPED ON IT.*

The Bible-Truth that God poured out the fullness of His wrath on His own Son, instead of mankind, reveals both that He loved His creation, and that *mankind was faced with problems IT COULD NOT NEGOTIATE ON ITS OWN—SIN AND CURSES-GALORE!* If mankind had not desperately needed deliverance from sin and its *MANY*-unpleasant-consequences, then Christ bore them all in vain! For, Paul said in Galatians 2:21: *"If righteousness comes BY* [us keeping] *the law, CHRIST DIED IN VAIN."* In modern-jargon: *"If WE could have repaired OUR own brokenness, then heaven BUTTED IN on our affairs for NO-VALID-REASON!* Had we human beings been *SELF-REDEEMING,* there would have been no reason for God to become a man, to take away burdens we *supposedly* were not able to bear. But I have already demonstrated from both the Bible and abundant-historical-proof that man is hopeless without God. Therefore,...

ONLY BY our acknowledging that we cannot make it without God will we grasp our need for redemption, and believe the Gospel-message about receiving redemption. ONLY IF we know that our selfish-lifestyle is leading us toward destruction will we call upon the Lord for mercy, and obtain our desperately-needed-deliverance!

However, people in general generally-refuse to admit there could be *ANYTHING* wrong with them personally. (Bible-proof—Proverbs 12:15, 16:2, 20:6, 21:2, 30:12.) Their problems might be somebody else's fault; but not their own! Pointing the finger-of-blame at the other guy began with Adam and Eve in the Garden of Eden—and most people hold to that Edenic-Sin as a human-right! (Genesis 3:12-13, 4:9, 1 Peter 1:18-19)

Mankind might spruce up its outside, and attempt to deceive itself and others about its actual-condition—but blinding oneself to the truth does not change the truth! It only adds to those spiritual-miles one must backtrack to arrive where he or she began to VEER OFF THE TRUTH. THE BEST MOVE IS TO AGREE WITH GOD UP FRONT! (Isaiah 30:18, 48:17-19, Jeremiah 29:11-13, Malachi 3:13-18) God's obey-now-or-pay-later-law.

What Scripture reveals about *ALL* that is involved in our redemption in Christ will likely *shock* the religious-crowd—but *pleasantly-surprise* the open-minded-folks. *Jesus paid an extreme-price to purchase redemption for believers.* Bible-Truth about *identification with Christ* is nothing like *religious-tradition*—guaranteed! That truth *BELIEVED AND ACTED UPON* revolutionizes one's life.

Ponder this precept: *The depth of man's degeneracy determined the sum of the Savior's sufferings in behalf of humanity; which inherited its hideous-habits from its first-father—Adam! In purchasing salvation, Christ had to become everything the fallen-Adam had become; plus suffer all the sufferings attached to his fallen-nature!*

The first-installment on the enormous-cost of man's redemption was *God Himself becoming a man—Miracle of miracles!* Another was Christ putting up with fallen-people's ill-manners for 33 years. (Matthew 17:17) And finally, the cross-cost—which Jesus Christ paid in full! (Isaiah 53, 1 Peter 2:24, etc.) But first things first,...

Almighty God became a human being; *SO THAT* His redemptive-activities on earth would be both legal and binding. *God promised in* Genesis 3:15 *that the Seed of the woman* (who would necessarily be a human) *would in due time crush the Serpent's head—Satan's authority gained over the entire-human-race through Adam's sin.* Although the verse does not establish the fact that the Seed would also be one member of the Godhead, other Bible-passages do. *In* Genesis 22:8, *Abraham told Isaac that God would provide HIMSELF a lamb for that burnt-offering—DOUBLE-REFERENCE—*pointing to what God did for Abraham that day, and prophesying the future-Christ-event. Abraham spotted a *RAM* entangled in the bushes, and offered it instead of Isaac. And, John 1:14 says clearly that the *Word*, Who was *God*, became flesh (man). Galatians 4:4 confirms that: "God sent forth His Son, made of woman, made under the law." "The *MAN*, Christ Jesus." (1 Timothy 2:5) God Himself descended to this planet as a humble-human. Another witness is Ezekiel 34:11-16, where God promised that He Himself would come and seek for the lost, bind up the injured, heal the sick, and judge between sheep and sheep.

A primary-passage is Hebrews 2:14: "Forasmuch as the children [Adam's descendants] partake of flesh and blood, He [God's Word] also Himself *LIKEWISE* partook of flesh and blood—that by means of His own death He [Jesus] might *destroy* [literal Greek—*render-ineffective*] the one that had the power [force] of death; that is, the devil." Genesis 3:15 said fallen-man's-problems would be remedied by a man (a human being): *But that could be achieved ONLY BY SOMEONE NOT BOUND BY SIN!* Since *ALL* of Adam's race was under sin and Satan, no one in Adam's race was qualified to do that redeeming! God had redeeming-*POWER*, but not *AUTHORITY* to do the redeeming—because He had delegated all authority over earth to man—who was now sinful—and therefore disqualified. The Divine-solution was for God (Who had power to redeem, but not authority, as God) *to become a man Who was not fallen; and so not under the devil's dominion.* Jesus Christ was that unique-man! And, the Bible fully-proves that truth! Also think about this,...

God breaking into this earth-realm *AS DEITY* would have *VIOLATED* His own rules: For He had given Adam the authority and responsibility to guard that paradise from God's enemy—Satan! (Genesis 1:26-28, 2:15) But rather than standing his ground, Adam actually joined ranks with God's enemy—which is when Satan became the "*god-of-this-age.*" (2 Corinthians 4:4) So, God came as a sinless-man and did the job Adam failed at. Jesus Christ was that man. The-ingenious-Divine-plan!

That was the Lord's introduction to earth; but what about His *preparation* for that event? Philippians 2:5-8 is Paul's explanation: "Christ Jesus: *being in the FORM of God, thought it not robbery to be equal with God: But, made Himself of no reputation, taking upon Himself the form of a servant; being made in the LIKENESS of men.*"

"Making Himself of no reputation" meant that Christ divested Himself of all Divine-attributes—*omnipotence, omniscience, and omnipresence. He depended on Holy-Spirit-power to do His miraculous-works: Certain facts He knew not about* (only the Father did): *And, He could be present in only one place at a time.* (Matthew 12:28, Mark 13:32, John 11:21) The Savior did not operate on earth *AS GOD; BUT AS MAN*—providing an example of what God expects of *ALL OF US* who are in Christ.

Hebrews 10:5 quotes Psalms 40:6-8 from the Greek rendering of the Old Testament—the Septuagint. *It is a prophecy of God preparing a body for the One Who was to bring salvation to all men.* To be legal, *redemption for mankind had to be procured by someone with a human body.* But, *that body had to be occupied by a spirit that was untainted by sin—one made of flesh, but without a human father—generated from above.* The Creator had deposited *PART* of Himself into Adam in the beginning (Genesis 2:7); so was the One Being most like Adam in *SUBSTANCE* (made in God's image); *thus, would be the most reasonable One to become a sacrifice to restore the fallen-human-race.* (Romans 8:3) But not so simple,...

Because, the primary-problem facing the Triune-God was Adam's sinful-nature. Even after becoming a man, the Word-made-flesh never sinned. (Hebrews 4:15) But Adam, and his descendants, whom Jesus Christ came to earth to redeem, had sinned. Moreover, not only had man *COMMITTED SIN*; Scripture says that *MAN IS SIN!* *"ALL UNRIGHTEOUSNESS IS SIN."* (1John 5:17) Thus, *UNRIGHTEOUSNESS* and *SIN* are *INTERCHANGEABLE-TERMS. "The UNRIGHTEOUS* [unsaved] *will NOT inherit the Kingdom of God."* (1 Corinthians 6:9) Fallen-man is tagged *UNRIGHTEOUS*; and even *UNRIGHTEOUSNESS!* Therefore, *WHEN JESUS WAS MADE TO BE SIN* (on the

cross—2 Corinthians 5:21)—what Adam had become—
THE SAVIOR HIMSELF BECAME UNRIGHTEOUSNESS!
Remember, sin *IS* unrighteousness! That means Jesus
Christ became fallen-Adam on that tree! More proof,...

"Be not unequally-yoked-together with *unbelievers*:
For, what fellowship has *righteousness* [believers] with
unrighteousness [unbelievers]?" "And what communion
has *light* with *darkness?*" "What agreement has *Christ*
with *Belial* [the devil]?" "What part has *he who believes*
with an *infidel* [unbeliever]?" "What agreement has the
temple of God with *idols? For, you are the temple of the
Living-God.*" (2 Corinthians 6:14-16) Exact-proof,...

"The *first-man* Adam became a living-soul [Genesis
2:7]; whereas the *LAST-ADAM* [Jesus Christ] became a
Life-Giving-Spirit." (1 Corinthians 15:45) *Christ on that
cross was called the LAST-ADAM!* And last means last!
"In Adam all die. In Christ all will be made alive [in the
new-birth and the resurrection]." (1 Corinthians 15:22)
*Jesus was the LAST-ADAM for just a short-time—on the
cross and down in Hades—three days and nights.* Then
He became that Second-Man through His resurrection.
(1 Corinthians 15:47) But, how did it start on earth,...

Luke wrote that *the angel Gabriel visited the young-
virgin-Mary with the startling-news that she was God's
chosen-vessel to bring the Messiah into this world.* But,
Mary's ignorance of *THE TECHNICALITIES* of that task
(she *NOT* having had *SEXUAL-RELATIONS* with a man)
elicited this response from the angel Gabriel: "*The Holy
Spirit will come upon you, and the power of the Highest
will overshadow you: Therefore, that holy thing that will
be born of you WILL BE called the Son of God.*" WILL BE
called God's Son; *NOT* has always been called His Son!
See Luke 1:26-38 for the full-account of that event.

What about Christ's abbreviated-existence *AS THE LAST-ADAM?* In 1 Corinthians 15:45-47, Paul referred to Genesis 2:7; *linking Adam's creation with the Christ-event*: *"The first-man Adam was made a living-soul; the LAST-ADAM was made a quickening [life-giving-]spirit."* (15:45) Verse-forty-seven then identifies the Last-Adam as "The Lord from heaven." *WHEREAS the apostle Paul TWICE-CALLED Adam THE FIRST-MAN, he IDENTIFIED Jesus ONCE AS THE LAST-ADAM, and ONCE AS THE SECOND-MAN—but NEVER the last-man or the second-Adam!* So, Jesus existed in two-different-states in that event—*Last-Adam and Second-Man. The Lord BECAME the LAST-SPECIMEN of one species of MAN, and FIRST-SPECIMEN of a new-species of MAN*—a new-creation:

"If any man is in Christ he is a NEW-CREATURE." (2 Corinthians 5:17) *The Greek word new in new-creature refers to the kind of being not existing before*—denoting *QUALITY—not quantity; TYPE—not number.* If Paul had called Christ the *Second-Adam,* he would have meant He was just one more of Adam's offspring. But, *by Paul designating the resurrected-Christ the Second-Man, he meant a totally-different-kind-of-man—a new-creature!*

Romans 5:14 says that Adam was "The figure [type] of Him [Christ] Who was to come." How was Adam the *type* of Christ? Adam was a sinner; Jesus was not—big difference! Moreover, *Adam fell from his God-ordained-position, whereas Christ obeyed His Father's command to come to the earth and carry out His redemption-plan. Through rebellion, Adam became a spiritual-child of the devil, whereas Christ said the prince of this world* (the devil) *owned nothing in Him.* John 14:30: *"The prince of this world comes, BUT HE HAS NOTHING IN ME."* The Amplified-Bible brings out the *RICHNESS* of the Greek-language involved in that statement by Jesus. So,...

What did Paul mean when he said in Romans 5:14 that *Adam was a TYPE OF CHRIST? The only similarity between the two was that, both Adam and Christ were the head of a race of people.* Adam, the original-head of man, *occasioned the fall of the entire-race by means of his sin.* Christ, on the other hand, *became the Head of a brand new race of people by rendering sin ineffective!* Paul taught that Jesus Christ was the first-fruit of the resurrection. (1 Corinthians 15:20) In other words, our Lord became the first-new-creature—the first of a new-kind-of mankind! *One more truth on the Last-Adam,...*

Most scholars misunderstand 1 Corinthians 15:45-47. Misquotes founded upon a *LACK OF STUDY* of that passage abound in footnotes of many reference-Bibles. Well-educated and well-respected preachers call Christ the *Second-Adam*—which is either a careless-oversight on their part; or mere speculation—because there is no *Second-Adam* appearing in Greek in that passage. The GREEK rendered in ENGLISH "The *first-man Adam*" is: *Protos anthropos Adam.* And "The *Last-Adam*": *Eskatas Adam.* "The *Second-Man*": *Deuteros anthropos. Second* and *Adam* do not occur together in that Greek text!

Am I just being *PICKY* over that issue; or is there a truth here we need to know? People who contend that Jesus was the *Second-Adam* obviously believe that He became such *when Mary conceived Him.* Had that been the case, Christ would have been the Second-Adam all His life. And, if that were true, *there were two different Adams co-existing upon this terrestrial-ball at the same time for thirty-three-years*—two competing Adams—one *a sinner by nature; the other sinless.* In God's creation-order, people came from the original-Adam only! Thus, *Jesus Christ could not have been some different-Adam; violating God's unalterable-creation-order!*

That distorted-view of Jesus implies as well that He would remain the *Second-Adam* for all eternity. *If such were the actual-case, what became of the FIRST-Adam? To where did the sinning-Adam go? And why did Jesus come to earth in the first place?* The first-Adam was the one who had insurmountable-problems—and the Word was made flesh to solve those problems. *God could not legally eliminate Adam's trouble by setting sinful-Adam aside.* Rather than replacing Adam, *Christ became one with sinful-Adam on the cross, in order to deliver sinful-Adam from sinful-Adam—so that people in Christ would become a new-kind-of-people! The Divine-solution!*

Our Savior abolishing Adam's sin-nature could not occur until God was ready to *GET RID OF* sinful-Adam. And that happened on the cross, at the very end of the Savior's mission on the earth; not in the womb of Mary at the beginning of His existence as a human being. He had other accomplishments to accomplish before going to the cross; *where He died as the Last-Adam! Then He was resurrected as the Second-Man.* By means of that sacrifice, *Jesus solved mankind's total-sin-problem and reduced the devil's hold on well-informed and obedient-believers to zero! We partake of the salvation our Savior purchased by becoming one with Christ in a new-birth.* (John 3:3, Romans 6:10-11, 1 Corinthians 15:22)

Had our Savior failed to redeem any part of human existence, the devil could lure even believers into those areas *not covered by Christ's sacrifice*, and prevent our reception of desperately-needed-benefits.

Moreover, had our Savior's sacrifice dealt only with *symptoms*, leaving the *root-problems* intact, our enemy would still have a stranglehold, even on believers. *But, because of the thoroughness of God's redemption-plan, the devil has absolutely no authority over well-informed and obedient-Christians! To defeat people in Christ, the devil would have to defeat Christ Himself,* and that will *NEVER* happen! (Luke 10:19, Romans 8:32, Colossians 1:13, James 4:7, 1 Peter 5:7-9, 1 John 5:18) Truth,...

Man's problems were not just *out there somewhere!* They were on the inside of him! To achieve an effective-redemption, *Christ had to strike at the ROOT of human-problems—man's spiritual-union with Satan!* But, those annoying-symptoms of sin were eliminated in the same sacrifice. Such is the genius of the Gospel! Our sinful-nature and all of sin's-consequences were destroyed by Christ's death on that cross; and His resurrection. *The sin-manufacturing-part of us has been eliminated*: "Old things have passed away, and *ALL* things have become new." (2 Corinthians 5:17) Moreover, God did not leave Christians in a spiritual-vacuum. Our salvation is both devoid of sin, and all its trappings, and filled with new-living-experiences in Christ—Godly experiences!

The old-things connected to the devil and our sinful-self are gone, and all things are new in Christ. And, *"all those new things are of God."* (2 Corinthians 5:18) That being the case, *we in Christ are not obligated to sign for any evil-packages the devil tries to deliver!* (James 4:7)

The next chapter is *a detailed-Bible-account* of what God's Beloved Son obtained for the entire-human-race *by His sufferings on the cross, and by what He endured down in Hades during those three days and nights He was there—and, of course, by His spiritual-resurrection from Hades, and His bodily-resurrection from the grave.*

Chapter Eleven

Total-redemption-package

Even though Jesus purchased and made accessible to this entire-human-race a complete-remedy for every human-predicament, *MOST* people do not want to hear about it. Multitudes think there is nothing wrong with *THEM* personally. In fact, *they become offended at the suggestion that their LIFESTYLE could be their primary-disability! MOST insist it is people harassing them who need ALL the adjustments.* They are satisfied with their life the way it is—except for physical-aches-and-pains, body-flab, nosy-neighbors, bill-collectors, and city-hall. They perceive not that to other people, they themselves just might be some of those nosy-neighbors, etc.

Christ offered Himself a WHOLE-SACRIFICE for the WHOLE-MAN—for every part of every person as well as every person. Our Savior slighted no country, century, or individual in providing redemption. *Jesus knew that when He began that cross-project, He would be bearing the entire-sin-load and curse-load of this entire-planet; providing complete-redemption for everyone on it.* (John 1:29-30, Hebrews 2:10, 1 John 2:2) Hebrews 2:9 says *"He came to taste death for every man."* That does not mean Christ came just to experience what *DEATH* was like. Rather, because death, *temporal* and *eternal*, was staring all of us right in our faces, our Savior came to destroy that destroyer. (2 Timothy 1:10, Hebrews 2:14) Thus, rejecting Divine-redemption *SEALS* one's *DOOM*; because redemption has *NO*-other-source. (John 3:36, 14:6, Acts 4:12, Romans 10:9-10, Hebrews 2:3-4) So, it is no big surprise that,...

Romans 5:6-10 tells us *those OUTSIDE of Christ fall into at least one of three less-than-desirable-categories: UNGODLY, SINNERS or ENEMIES* of God. That passage does not refer only to especially-evil-characters. All the unsaved fit into one or more of those slots. But,...

Every human being on earth is a *potential-recipient* of the salvation our Lord purchased by His crucifixion, death, burial and resurrection! *That naturally includes aborted-babies. There is biblical and scientific-evidence that the unborn are human even before they reach full-term* (even at conception). *If not, the pre-maturely-born would not be human either!* Check out Psalms 139:13-16, Jeremiah 1:5 and Romans 7:9. Thus, *abortion after conception is the termination of a human being!*

That redemption our Savior accomplished is more-far-reaching in both *SCOPE* and *DEPTH* than religious-tradition allows. *Denominational-adherents are shallow and narrow-minded. If they dare deal with the human-predicament at all, they approach only the sin-part of it.* MOST theologians neither believe nor teach that *Christ came to rescue man from sin's temporal-consequences, as well as eternity in Hades!* They even shun the Bible-Truth that, by means of that sacrifice, *Christ provided all who BELIEVE with DIVINE-RIGHTEOUSNESS; which reverses their previous-UNRIGHTEOUS-state-of-being!*

The truth is: *Not only did sin do damage to the spirit of lost-people; it also occasioned painful and degrading-afflictions in the bodies of lost-people* (AND unbelieving-believers'-bodies as well). Romans 5:12 tells us *DEATH was introduced on earth through Adam's sin. But death manifests itself on earth in different forms and degrees*: Poverty, depression, illness, pain, and other *EVILS* that many consider to be *NORMAL* today. Beyond that,...

More and more human beings today seem compelled by their spiritual-union with Satan to commit all-kinds-of-unimaginable-evil (Genesis 6:5, John 8:44, Romans 1:18-32, Ephesians 2:2, 1 John 3:8, 5:19); *proving the truthfulness of the Bible-Account! Now this truth,...*

DEATH being the direct-result of SIN (Romans 5:12), *BOTH SIN AND DEATH ARE ENEMIES of both the saved and unsaved.* (1 Corinthians 15:26) *But what is death? DEATH IS ULTIMATE-WEAKNESS.* Envision a line with *SIN* to begin, and *DEATH* at the other end. Sin *BEGINS* one's downward-progression toward ultimate-death. *In ultimate-death one is not able to PERFORM—even to the LEAST degree. Yet LESSER-forms and degrees of death exist between the two ends of that line—Pains that are not death in its fullness, but ARE LIFE-LIMITING—*often bringing afflicted-ones to full-death—*LIFE-CEASING.*

Poverty is definitely a form and degree of *weakness;* and *extreme-poverty eventually produces STARVATION.* Disease also *weakens the physical body;* and if disease is not eliminated, *it produces DEATH.* Depression leads the depressed to contemplate *suicide*—a common-form of *DEATH.* So death is not always instantaneous: *Often it comes in installments!* Scripture informs us,...

Our Creator was SO concerned about BOTH sin and death that He sent His Son to this world to destroy both of those ENEMIES. So, is it not reasonable to believe as well that God planned to do away with all the *LESSER-DEGREES* of death? If He desired the *CAUSE* of death (*SIN*) and the final-*END* of sin (*DEATH*) to be destroyed, He would surely want all the lesser-forms and degrees of death to be eliminated along with them! *Why would God erase sin from one end of that line, and death from the other, but leave all the intermediate-pains intact?*

God desires not that His faithful-people tolerate sin or any related-curses in their lives. As a matter of fact, both Romans 6:18 and Galatians 3:13 tell us that we have been *FREED* from both sin and all those curses!

As Jesus Christ was suspended upon those wooden beams, *He dealt with every-existing-human-problem!* (2 Corinthians 5:21, Galatians 3:13-14, 2 Timothy 1:10, 1 Peter 2:24, Revelation 1:5) What were the problems?

Deuteronomy 28:15-68 *pertains not to sin but to the CURSES resulting from sin. Moses warned the Israelites that if they did not obey God's every-command all those curses would eventually come upon them and overtake them because of their disobedience.* But Galatians 3:13 says JESUS REDEEMED US BELIEVERS FROM EVERY-CURSE recorded in Deuteronomy 28:15-68. Notice,...

Deuteronomy 28:15-68 catalogs about every kind of physical-ailment; including *consumption* (tuberculosis), *inflammation* (arthritis), *sore boils* (infection), (partial or total) *blindness, heart-failure,* (every kind of) *fever,* and *mental-disorders*; to name only a few. And just in case anyone fails to realize that God declared *ALL* physical-ailments to be curses, Moses added in verse-sixty-one: "Also *EVERY* sickness and *EVERY* plague, which is not written in the book of the law [plus all those that are]." *That means no pain or infirmity is a blessing!* Paul said in Galatians 3:13 that our Lord removed from believers *ALL* of those curses. How did He do it? *Buckle up your spiritual-seat-belt, and let us go for a Gospel-ride.* Since our Lord paid that blood-price to purchase redemptive-blessings for us, let us flex our study-muscles, to learn about that redemption our Savior wrought for us upon that chunk of wood. So here we go on that eye-opening Gospel-journey! It will be a life-changer for many.

Matthew 8:17: "[Christ] *Himself took* [upon Himself] *our infirmities and bore* [removed] *our sicknesses." And that was as much a part of His tasting death for every man as was His being made SIN!* (2 Corinthians 5:21, Hebrews 2:9) *Our Lord was never sick until He became sick with OUR sicknesses on the cross.* And, He bore all those infirmities within His own being to heal all of us who believe that part of His sacrifice. Romans 10:9-10 says if we believe with our heart that God raised Christ from the dead, and confess with our mouth that Jesus is Lord, we will be *SAVED. The English word SAVED or salvation, from the Greek soozoo, is all-inclusive. Bible-dictionaries PROVE that the Greek word soozoo means RESCUE FROM ANY FORM OF DANGER; be it spiritual, material, moral, physical, financial, or ANY threatening-circumstance.* Religion teaches that our Savior rescued believers *ONLY* from the *FUTURE*-consequence of sin—Hades; and maybe some of our present-guiltiness. But, *God's Word is CLEAR that Christ delivered us from sin's EVERY-RESULT—FUTURE and PRESENT!* Jesus having saved us from sin's ultimate-consequences, why would He want us to continue suffering the partial-ones?

Matthew 8:17 clarifies the Hebrew in Isaiah 53:4-5: *Griefs* and *sorrows* in the King James Bible are rightly-rendered *diseases* and *physical-pains—from which we were healed—verse-five—the same Hebrew word for the HEALING of diseases throughout the Old Testament.* In Luke 5:23, Jesus asked: "Which is easier *TO SAY* [to a paralyzed-man]: 'Your sins be forgiven you'; or 'Rise up [completely-healed] and walk'?" *The healing of sickness is no more difficult than is the forgiveness of one's sins.* Moreover, *Christ dealt with illness with no-less-urgency than He did sins—delivering every sufferer, who asked Him in faith for help*—alleviating every manifestation of the curse. *And Jesus came to do and teach God's will!*

Isaiah 53:4: *"SURELY, [Christ] HAS BORNE [as His own ALL of] our griefs [Hebrew—choliy—diseases], and CARRIED [away ALL of] our sorrows [Hebrew—makob—pains]." Christ took ALL those CURSES upon Himself, in order to RID US believers of them ALL!* Galatians 3:13: *Christ redeemed us from the curses of the law* (poverty, sickness, etc.) *BY becoming a curse—just as He saved us from sin by becoming sin!* (2 Corinthians 5:21)

Deuteronomy 28:47-48: *The curse of POVERTY robs us of necessities and our personal-dignity.* Jesus *BORE* our *POVERTY as well.* "You know the grace of our Lord Jesus Christ, that though He was rich [before He hung on the cross], yet for your sake He became poor [on the cross], so that you, through His poverty, might become rich." (2 Corinthians 8:9) *Christ BECAME POOR WITH OUR POVERTY at the same time and place HE BECAME SIN WITH OUR SINS* and *SICK WITH OUR SICKNESSES* (on the cross); rendering them all invalid in the lives of people who dare to believe in and confess that portion of the Inspired-Redemption-Truth of God's Word.

The claim that Jesus Christ became *POOR* when He left heaven, and was born on earth, is a religious-error! *How many POOR-KIDS HAVE THREE-RICH-KINGS visit them from some foreign-nation, bringing them precious-metal and expensive-perfume, while snubbing the ruler of that kingdom? And, do you believe Joseph and Mary kept that gold, frankincense and myrrh on the fireplace-mantle, as family-heirlooms—or, put those valuables to practical-uses?* The Heavenly-Father was taking care of His Son on earth—even from birth! (Matthew 2:13-15) *God knew that Christ's family would need some extra-cash to fund that unplanned-journey to Egypt and back.* And, Jesus was born in a stable because all the motel-rooms had been rented out already. (Luke 2:7)

Carpenter's-sons were not raised in abject-poverty! Jews who had a business or skilled-trade were not the poor of Israel. Neither did Christ's ministry-staff suffer from poverty. *Several women of considerable-financial-means funded Christ's miracle-campaigns.* (Luke 8:2-3) Moreover, *Christ's ministry got so large that He needed a treasurer to handle the cash-flow; and the money-box had enough in it to constantly give to the plentiful-poor, and the treasurer—Judas—was a thief, helping himself to some of those funds.* (John 12:6, 13:29) Our Savior supported eighty-two other preachers, besides Himself; plus their families! And He fed thousands of people out in the wilderness. I would not say one who could afford that kind of ministry was poor. More Bible-Proof,...

In Luke 4:18, *Jesus said He had come to preach the Gospel to the poor!* Did Christ preach to Himself? Had He been poor, such would have required that He do so! And in another passage *He settled once and for all the question of whether He was poor prior to hanging upon that impoverishing-cross.* When His disciples scolded a woman for wasting expensive-ointment BY POURING IT ALL UPON HIM, Jesus responded: "You have the POOR with you always, and whensoever you will, you may do THEM [poor-ones] good: BUT ME you have not always." (Matthew 26:11, Mark 14:7, John 12:8) Thus, Christ's own testimony proves that HE WAS NOT POOR prior to the cross. If you can envision our Savior nailed to that rugged-piece-of-timber; and His life-blood spurting out on the ground; the soldiers gambling for the last of His earthly-possessions, and a heartless-mob cursing Him, while He bore their curses for them, then you may see an-impoverished-Savior. Christ suffered poverty *ONLY* on the cross; *and the only reason He became poor then was to deliver you and me from poverty—the same way He delivered us from sin and all the other curses!*

Apart from Christ's *redemptive-sufferings*, there are no *redemptive-blessings*. Other than the benefits of the natural-creation (*all of which are under sin's curse*), no blessings are available to people; except what our Lord purchased upon the cross. *But, most of those blessings belong to us believers right now during this-age!*

Can believers experience heaven in this-present-age; or, are deceased-believers barred from heaven until the next-dispensation? Dead-Christians' spirits do not float around in the atmosphere until Jesus returns. Neither do they experience *soul-sleep*, as some want to believe. *At our bodily-passing, we Christians enter the presence of our Lord in heaven.* (2 Corinthians 5:8) Indeed, most of what our Lord purchased on the cross belongs to us now; including heaven, as we *EXIT* this world! *The only exception to those blessings we may receive during this-life is the resurrection of our body—which we will all get at the same time. But, before we EXIT, Christ ministers the Gospel to and through our un-resurrected-bodies!*

Moreover, Christ's own Father forsook Him when He became the Last-Adam on that cross (Matthew 27:46); *in order to pay for the blessing of God not forsaking us.* (Hebrews 13:5) Christ also said in Mark 10:33-34 that He would be *subjected to shame*, to deliver us believers from shame. (Romans 9:33, 10:11) Christ shrank from no hardship placed upon Him while on that cross. Had He left anything *UNDONE*, Satan would still have some *LEVERAGE*, even against New-Testament-believers!

Most Christians believe that Jesus bore our sins on the cross, but many struggle with the Bible-Truth that our Savior healed our bodies, as well. *Most believe that healing is a sovereign-act-of-God.* When somebody gets healed through *Bible-Faith*, most contend that it is just their time to get healed anyway; or that they are one of the lucky-ones; or they have a super-faith, which most Christians should not expect to possess. Of course, to people with that mindset, *Divine-prosperity is out of the question.* Money being worldly, *we ought not CHEAPEN the Gospel by making finances PART of our redemption. Religion has EMASCULATED the Gospel of both Divine-healing and Divine-provision.* But 2 Corinthians 8:9-12 tells us that *Divine-prosperity was secured by Christ's sacrifice on the same cross where He took upon Himself our SINS and SICKNESSES. Christ wrought redemption for every man and every part of every man on that tree!*

That Greek word rendered *REDEEMED* in Galatians 3:13 means *to buy up all there is to buy. Was man only partially-lost; or was he totally-lost?* If Christ's sacrifice had failed to cover even the minutest-details of Adam's lost-blessings (including every body part), *then the new earth will be populated by less-than-whole-inhabitants*; because many will be beheaded during the Tribulation; and *ONLY* what Jesus redeemed will be included in the resurrection—restoration of the entire-individual!

By becoming the Last-Adam, Christ bore more than man himself. One *BIG* problem was Adam's union with the devil through sin: So, *Christ identified with Adam's UNION with the devil!* (John 3:14) *That revelation butts heads with religious-tradition, but that deliverance was a necessary part of God's overall-redemption-plan.* The cross separated Adam's family from Satan's-dominion. (Colossians 1:13, Hebrews 2:14, 1 John 3:8) Jesus had to cover it all, or forget the whole thing. He covered it!

The Savior, referring to Numbers 21:8-9, said about Himself in John 3:14 that: "Just as Moses lifted up the Serpent in that wilderness, even so [for that very same purpose] must the Son of man be lifted up [crucified]."

Out in the wilderness, *Moses fastened onto a pole a bronze-replica of a snake.* Bronze represents judgment: So that hanging-serpent represented a judged-serpent; whose poison had been neutralized—*so Israel's snake-bitten-murmurers would be SAVED from deadly-poison by gazing on that judged-serpent—which was a type of Christ on the cross—WHO judged the real-Serpent—the devil.* If those Israelite-repenters were *HEALED* in their bodies by gazing upon the type of Christ, then trusting in the *REAL*-Christ will surely *HEAL* our bodies today!

Isaiah 52:14: "His *VISAGE* was so disfigured [on the cross], *MORE* than any man, and His *FORM* disfigured *MORE* than the sons of men." *Many theologians believe that verse portrays the physical-torment Christ suffered before He was crucified*; claiming it refers to the stripes Jesus sustained at the Roman-whipping-post. *Not so!*

The Savior was disfigured not in His body; for John said that prophecy: *"A bone of Him will not be broken."* referred to the Lord's cross-experience. (Exodus 12:46, Numbers 9:12, Psalms 34:20, John 19:33-36) *Though some insist His body became disfigured while darkness covered the earth for three hours during His crucifixion; claiming that since it was pitch-dark during that time no one could see what was happening on the cross*—Even that belief rejects the claim that the stripes from man's whip wrought our healing. Did our Lord's body become disfigured during that darkness, then return to normal when the sky cleared again? Both Matthew 27:54 and Luke 23:44-49 provide eyewitness-accounts of several people beholding that entire-event. *The Roman-soldiers were responsible for keeping tabs on Christ throughout the entire-ordeal, so we can be sure they were attentive to all that happened to Christ's body.* (Matthew 27:36) Besides, *what purpose would it serve to disfigure Jesus in the darkness, then restore Him as the light returned?*

Moreover, our resurrected-Savior displayed *SCARS ONLY from those wounds inflicted upon His body in the crucifixion—nail-prints and one spear-gash.* He showed no scars in connection with disfiguring on the cross. If His flesh suffered the contortions mentioned in Isaiah 52:14, why was His resurrected-body not scarred from being marred? Jesus suffered all of that in His spirit!

This planet knew no sickness until sin came in. *Sin being spiritual in nature, sickness, which sin introduced to earth, is spiritual in nature, as well.* Sickness, having *spiritual-roots*, its logical-cure must be *spiritual-power*. Our Savior used spiritual-power to heal sick bodies on earth, and *He operates* the same today! (Matthew 8:16-17, 1 Corinthians 12:28, James 5:14-16, 1 Peter 2:24)

Did those Roman soldiers place our sins on Jesus? *They had NO ACCESS to the sins of the world.* God did! *Men made not our Lord sick with our sicknesses either. A man might infect others with disease-germs, but only God could put our diseases on Jesus in such a way as to REDEEM US from them.* God gathered up every vile-sin, every putrid-sickness, and poverty too, and placed them all on His Son on the cross—all at the same time. *Jesus suffered bodily by men's HANDS, but He purchased redemption through His spiritual-sufferings under His Father's HANDS!* (Isaiah 53:4-5, 10, Matthew 8:17, 2 Corinthians 8:9, 1 Peter 2:24, etc.) Realize this,...

The disciples did not see all their sins, diseases and poverty being placed on Christ. *All they saw with their natural-eyes was their ONLY-HOPE being stripped from them by a cruel-instrument-of-torture*—whereas Jewish-religious-leaders *ASSUMED* that they were finally being relieved of their-most-dreaded-foe—Truth. Even Satan did not understand what was going on. (1 Corinthians 2:8) Only God knew what was being accomplished!

It would seem enough that heartless-Roman-soldiers crucified Him, jealous-Jewish-leaders jeered at Him, an angry-mob mocked Him, and all His friends abandoned Him—but He was forsaken by His Heavenly Father too! (Matthew 27:46) *Zechariah 13:7 prophesied that God would smite the Shepherd and scatter the sheep.* Jesus quoted that in Matthew 26:31. *It was God Who SMOTE the Shepherd—not men: So, it was what God did to His Beloved Son, which purchased our redemption; not what men did to Him before, during or after the cross.*

One more accomplishment was necessary, however. Christ bore within Himself all sins, sicknesses, poverty and other curses of this world. But, what would He do with all that junk? *Leviticus chapter-sixteen pictures it. Two goats were sacrificed on the yearly-Jewish-Day-of-Atonement.* One goat was slaughtered (pointing to the Lord's bodily-death); the other goat released *ALIVE* into the wilderness, after the high priest had laid his hands on the goat's head, confessing over it all of Israel's sins (picturing Christ's spiritual-descent into Hades). *Jesus prophesied He would be three days and three nights in the-earth's-core.* (Matthew 12:40) *His first-act upon His arrival there was to make that FINAL-PAYMENT for our sins, by suffering the Hades-judgment-part of it.*

But, Jesus had another reason for going to Hell: *To deposit EVERY sin and curse He had brought with Him into that wretched-place*; just as that scapegoat carried all of Israel's sins and curses into the wilderness. And, our Resurrected-Lord brought *NO SIN OR CURSE* back with Him to this living-realm. That means that we who are in Christ have been freed from the sins and curses He took with Him to Hades. It also means inhabiters of the Lake of Fire have nothing *GOOD* to look forward to: *GOOD THINGS* would be out of place in that place! *But repentance before death cancels the Hades-habitation!*

Chapter Twelve

No longer identified with Adam

The God behind that salvation-plan certainly could not abandon the plan's Price-Payer in that awful place; because man's-welfare was connected to the welfare of the very Son of God Himself. The genius of God's-plan was that, when our Lord was released from Hades (and sin and the curses), believers were delivered from all of them as well. *Our-deliverance was intricately-entwined with the-Savior's-deliverance—because His-deliverance is our-deliverance!* All that Christ achieved by means of His sacrifice He achieved for you and me. *Had the Lord been in need of salvation HIMSELF, He would not have been qualified to save anyone else. Jesus paid the due-penalty for our transgressions! He had none of His own!* (Hebrews 4:15) That being the case, there was no need for Christ to remain confined in Hell's-hot-hold.

God's Adversary, of course, desperately-desired that his *CONQUERER* remain entrapped in Hades. Once the Savior entered that underworld, if He could not escape that abode, humanity's eternal-fate would be sealed as well—*the devil would have all mankind locked into the destruction-mode.* While Satan does not own or control Hades, *knowing that fiery-furnace has been designated his eternal-dwelling-place, he wants ALL human beings to partake of it too!* So, he tries to herd them all in that direction. *Believers need to appreciate the fact that our-Savior's-VICTORY over the devil, sin, death, Hades and the grave was OUR-VICTORY over them too!* Had Christ not been able to escape Hades, it would be our eternal-abode as well. *But, Jesus paid our fare out of there!*

Colossians 2:15, in the King James Bible, says that our Lord "*SPOILED* principalities and powers." But, *the Greek verb rendered SPOILED is in the MIDDLE-VOICE, which literally indicates an action the subject performs upon himself, and not upon others.* It means *to disrobe.* Thus, our Lord acted not upon those principalities and powers, to strip something from them. No, *He disrobed Himself of them!* Got them off His back, so to speak. Of course, in doing so, He defeated them. Evidently, *those powers-of-darkness had planned to prevent Jesus from escaping that fire-pit.* The Creator of this universe was *THE PRIZE* they sought. *If the devil and his crew could somehow trap the Almighty Himself, mankind would be doomed too; and the Adversary's problems would all be solved—God's judgments would no longer be a threat to the devil, other fallen angels or demons.* (Matthew 8:29, Jude 6, Revelation 20:10) The devil did not know, until it was too late, however, that God had sprung His own trap—Christ on that cross. So, by engaging in their all-out-attempt to obtain a greater-trophy—the Son of God Himself—those powers-of-darkness lost the *PRIZE* they already had in hand—lost-man. *The devil and his band got defeated by God's-plan.* (Psalms 9:15-16, Proverbs 26:27, 1 Corinthians 2:6-8). Colossians 2:15 means,...

After His bearing all of this world's sins and curses, evil-entities attempted to keep our Savior's Spirit from escaping Hell. Christ broke free anyway: Which means that: Neither Satan nor any of his crew has power over any believer who knows the truth and is obedient to it. *By Christ dislodging those unclean-spirits from Himself, He established that no being has power over those who come into union with Christ through the new-birth!* HIS-*victory over demons and fallen angels was* OUR-*victory over the same. But, even though our Lord defeated them for us, they still exist, and still prowl around; and so we still have to resist their illegal-attacks against us!* (Mark 16:17, John 3:14, 12:31, 16:8-11, Acts 2:36, Romans 8:37-39, Colossians 1:12-13, 2:13-15, Hebrews 2:14, James 4:7, 1 Peter 5:8-9, 1 John 3:8, 5:4-5, 18)

Christ was put to death in His flesh, but made alive (in His Spirit) by the Holy Spirit. (1 Peter 3:18-19) And, Romans 4:25 says: "Christ was delivered [up by God to crucifixion] because of *OUR-OFFENSES* [against God]; and was raised again [in both spirit and body], in order to purchase *OUR-JUSTIFICATION.*" Which means that: When Christ was declared righteous, we were declared righteous; and when He was made alive, we were made alive *IN HIM!* Ephesians 2:5: We being dead in sin, *God made us ALIVE TOGETHER WITH CHRIST. So it is only IN CHRIST that we live and win in life!* (Romans 8:37)

After His Spirit was made alive in the *HEART* of this planet (Matthew 12:40), the Lord went and preached to the human spirits, fallen-angels, and demons confined in the underworld: Hades, Abraham's bosom, Paradise, Tartarus and the Abyss. (1 Peter 3:19) Jesus had more to do down-under than to suffer three days and nights. His body still dead in the grave, the moves Jesus made in that lower-realm were by His recreated-Spirit. While there, *He testified to each resident* (good and evil) *that God's prophecies had been fulfilled. That was an I-told-you-so-mission! Old-Covenant-SAINTS were vindicated for their trust in and obedience to the Creator, while the REBELS found their obstinacy HAD FAILED to override God's prophesied-judgments.* (2 Peter 2:4-9, Jude 6-7)

After the Lord had finished the *redemptive-work* His Father had sent Him to accomplish *on earth* and *in the bowels of it*, His Spirit was made alive (raised from the dead). Then, His resurrected-Spirit re-entered His body in the tomb, and made it alive again as well—thrusting His complete-resurrected-self out of the grave in glory: The greatest event in human-history! Prophecies of it:

Psalms 16:8-11 prophesied that the Savior's *FLESH* would *REST* in hope. So, *His sufferings after His death on the cross had to occur in His Spirit—not in His body!* Acts 2:24: Christ was *LOOSED* (set free from) the *pains* (as a woman in childbirth) *of death.* Those pains could not have occurred in His *DEAD-BODY* up in the tomb. Acts 2:27: "You will not leave My *SOUL* in Hell." Christ Himself declared that He would be in the heart (center) of the earth for three days and nights (Matthew 12:40); and this passage confirms that His *SOUL* was in Hades (abode of departed-spirits). Graves are not Hades-deep. Their bottom is usually about six feet below the earth's surface. So, Hell cannot possibly be the grave!

I have twenty-plus versions of the New Testament; and at least five of them have mistranslated the Greek word Hades as the *GRAVE. The context of several other New Testament Scriptures rules out any possibility that HADES refers to A HOLE IN THE DIRT on the surface of the earth.* The Lord prophesied that those Capernaum-citizens would someday be thrown into Hades, because most of them had refused to believe His message, even after He had performed many healing-miracles in their city. (Matthew 11:23) *If Hades means grave, that verse would suggest that believing-ones would not be buried!* And if Hades is the grave, those who are now buried in graves are in Hades. Hades is the underworld-abode of the wicked-dead—not a six-foot-deep-dirt-hole!

Luke 16:19-31 tells about a rich man who died and was *BURIED* (in a dirt-grave); but was surprised to find *HIMSELF ENGULFED IN THE FLAMES OF HADES.* Now, if Hades was the *GRAVE* in which the man's *BODY* had been laid to *REST*, had his grave been set on fire? Was it his *FLESH* that was burning? *The rich man also saw Lazarus and talked with Father-Abraham. Do cadavers converse with other cadavers BURIED next door?* These and other passages prove it preposterous to teach that Hades is just a hole people dig to put bodies in. *Graves are COOL—Hades is HOT!* Theological hypocrisy,...

MISTRANSLATING any word or passage of Scripture suggests that the Bible-translator is either incompetent, or dishonest—or both! Furthermore, *academic-infidelity regarding the clear-definition and usage of the original-Greek or Hebrew words in one Scripture passage raises a concern that there could be more manipulated-words elsewhere in that version.* So, doctorate-degrees are no guarantee of *HONESTY* in degree-holders! (Surprised?)

Jesus Christ was the Last-Adam three days or less. After completing His sin-bearing-mission, He rose from the dead and became *the-first-new-creature* of the New Testament—*which He purchased for the rest of us with His own shed-blood.* (Acts 20:28) Moreover, Acts 13:33 calls our Lord's resurrection a begetting! His Spirit was begotten (*REBORN*) in Hades. His body was not reborn: It was made alive and glorified. Nor does that Scripture refer to His birth in Bethlehem thirty-three-years back. Psalms 2:7-9 is a prophecy of Christ's *RESURRECTION* at the end of His mission here—not His baby-birth.

Jesus Christ is no longer identified with Adam! The Last-Adam *WAS* the *Last-Adam.* Consequently, *all who through faith have been united with Christ are relieved of Adam's sinful-nature too!* In God's Kingdom, Adam's sinful-race no longer exists. *BUT*, unrepentant-sinners will eternally inhabit Hades—unless they repent before it is too late. *AND THEY CAN REPENT!* See Acts 17:30.

Romans 6:6-7: *"Knowing that our OLD-MAN [self or sinful-nature] was crucified with Christ—that the body-of-sin [man's union with the devil through Adam] might be destroyed* [rendered ineffective]; *that henceforth, we* [believers] *should not serve* [be in bondage to] *sin. For, he who has died* [to sin WITH Christ in His crucifixion] *has been FREED FROM SIN* [both its guilt and power]." *Christ's-crucifixion was our-crucifixion; and His-release from identification with Adam was our-release from the same.* We cannot be God's child and the devil's child at the same time! (Matthew 6:24, John 8:44) Moreover,...

Romans 6:10: *"For, in that He* [Jesus Christ] *died, He died unto sin once* [and for all]: *But in that He lives, He lives unto God."* Verse-eleven: *"Likewise* [just as our Savior], *reckon* [count] *also yourselves to be dead unto sin, BUT alive unto God through Jesus Christ our Lord."*

To reckon means to put to one's account. Therefore, we are to count ourselves to be just as free from sin and spiritual-death as Christ is! "As He [Jesus Christ] is, *so are we believers in this world right now."* (1 John 4:17) Now, that is *REAL-BIBLE-IDENTIFICATION!* Our bodies not having been resurrected *YET*, 1 John 4:17 refers to our *spiritual-condition* in this-age. Romans 6:14 states: *"Sin will not have dominion over you* [during this-age]." Moreover, Jesus *abolished death* through His sacrifice. (2 Timothy 1:10) That has to mean spiritual-death, *for even Christian-bodies die before the resurrection.* When we finish our course in this life, we are to just drop our bodies and go home. For, to be absent from the body is to be present with the Lord. (2 Corinthians 5:6-8)

What about Satan? Was he affected by what Christ did upon the cross, and down in Hell? The Greek term *katargeoo* in Romans 6:6, 2 Timothy 1:10 and Hebrews 2:14 means to render *totally-ineffective. Through death, our Lord destroyed* (rendered totally-ineffective) *Satan, as well as sin and death.* The devil, sin, and death having become ineffective to us who believe, we have a *Divine-right* to refuse any curse the devil throws at us. For,...

Galatians 3:13 states: *"Christ has redeemed us from THE CURSE OF THE LAW."* So, according to Scripture, we believers have already been rescued out of the grip of Satan, sin, and *ALL* of sin's curses. Thus, in Christ, *we believers may finish our course on earth during this-evil-age, with God's blessings and protection—and then lay down these bodies and bask in our Lord's presence. Spiritual-death for the Christian is a thing of the past!* (John 6:50-51, 8:51, 10:28, 11:25-26) Also read again 2 Corinthians 5:6-8. Of course, we must realize,...

The devil did not go out of existence. *He still walks around, seeking someone to devour.* (1 Peter 5:8-9) But, *genuine-believers have been made off-limit to the devil and all of his junk.* Christ's sacrifice did not change the devil himself—he is still the same old Adversary—*but it did limit the scope of the territory he can do damage to.* He having no legal-right to damage or control genuine-believers, Satan uses deception to *LURE* believers away from God's Word—ignorantly or deliberately yielding to satanic-control—and he can *THEN* do damage to them. This book reveals biblical-weaponry, which overcomes all of the devil's deceptive and destructive-arsenal.

NONE of Christ's works were mere-merciful-acts-of-God. Each blessing Jesus ministered had to be paid for! Sins committed under the Old Covenant had not been removed. The blood of bulls and goats could never take away sin. *It just PROTECTED Old-Covenant-saints from God's judgment, until God's Word could be made flesh, and wash away those sins by God's blood.* (Acts 20:28, Romans 3:25, Hebrews 9:15, Revelation 1:5)

Luke 19:10: Jesus came to seek and save what was lost. Since every part of man was lost (spirit, soul, and body), whatever affected either our spirit, soul, or body had to be dealt with on the cross; or else the Savior did not finish the *WORK* His Father sent Him to do. Isaiah 55:10-11 says God's Word will not return to Him *VOID* (empty), but will achieve all that He sends it to achieve. So, *Jesus being God's WORD* (John 1:1, 14, Revelation 19:13), *by God's-OWN-RULE Jesus had to complete His mission—or else He could not have re-entered heaven!* Without fail, Christ fulfilled *EVERY-PROPHECY* related to His blood-sacrifice for mankind. Not only did Christ provide salvation for every-man—*He provided salvation for EVERY-PART of every-man*. And that means,...

It being our sins, sicknesses, poverty, curses, death and Hell that Christ bore in His sacrifice on our behalf, when He was *FREED* from *ALL* those evils, so were we! *Our sinful-nature was ELIMINATED, and the POISON of the Serpent on the pole was NEUTRALIZED.* (John 3:14, Galatians 3:13, Hebrews 2:14, 7:26) Therefore,...

When we, by faith and obedience, identify ourselves with the *crucified, having-died, buried, resurrected* and *ascended-Christ*, the same changes occurring in Christ also occur in our own inner-being! And because of that supernatural-deliverance from our old-sinful-nature by being united with Jesus Christ through our new-birth, God views and treats us just like He does Christ!

In the following chapter, we go into detail about the life-changing-experiences available to all who are fully-immersed-into, and continue to abide-in, Jesus Christ.

Chapter Thirteen

Death to our old-nature

The final-three-chapters of this book cover in detail the *HOW-TO* of becoming identified with Jesus Christ; to receive the redemption He purchased in our behalf. This, and the-following-two-chapters, identify who and what we *UNIDENTIFY WITH* and *IDENTIFY WITH*, upon our acceptance of Jesus as Savior—persons and things we become *SEPARATED FROM, AND UNITED TO*, when we get born again. That revelation will *SHIFT* religious-minds either into the denial-mode—or repentance, and acceptance of the salvation the Gospel provides. Yet,...

How can a *LOST-PERSON* embrace the resurrected-Christ—since Christ is no longer identified with sinful-Adam—*to whom all unsaved-characters are connected? Every unsaved-person being a descendant of Adam, ON WHAT BASIS CAN THEY TERMINATE THE SIN-NATURE THEY INHERITED FROM ADAM?* (Romans 5:12, 17-19, 1 Peter 1:18-19) You have to know the Bible-answer:

The answer being: *Salvation is not an add-on to our-old-sinful-existence. It is a total-exchange of personality and status: An exchange of masters and conditions. We must experience a major-spiritual-transformation on the inside of us.* Is it actually possible for one to experience that sort of alteration of his or her sinful-inner-nature? Yes! How? By becoming a new-creature, just like Jesus Christ did when He rose from the dead. *"If any man* [or woman] *be in Christ, he* [or she] *is a NEW-CREATURE."* (2 Corinthians 5:17) *Being a NEW-creature means one is no longer the OLD-creature he or she used to be!*

That verse goes on: "Old-things have passed away." Well, if all of the old-things of our past-lives are *GONE*, we are nothings; unless: "All things have become new." *The same changes which occurred in our Savior by His death, burial, and resurrection have to become our own experiences! They do in the new-birth—identifying with Jesus Christ in HIS death, burial and resurrection.*

Let us consider the biblical-view of three major areas of human-experience, wherein separation from our past is activated within us when we become a new-creature in Christ. Both our inner and outer-being are affected!

First is our separation from our *old-selfish-lifestyle. We used to do things our way. Nobody else could tell us what to do, or how to do it! We were OUR OWN BOSS; WE THOUGHT!* Isaiah 53:6: "*ALL of us like sheep have gone astray; we have turned each one to his own way.*" But *WHO* influenced us to turn! Other forces have had an influence in our life—either God, or the devil! (John 8:44, Romans 6:6, 11, 17-18, 1 John 5:19) Then,...

The second area of separation in our redemption is *OUR RESCUE* from Satan's control. *Adam's union with Satan gave Satan much CONTROL over mankind.* (John 8:44, Romans 5:12, 19, 2 Timothy 2:26, 1 John 5:19) Consequently, *many people* (*BOTH* saved and unsaved) *actually cooperate with their very own ENEMY, to bring about their very own DESTRUCTION!* So our-old-sinful-lifestyle and the devil's-dominion over us being closely-connected, the Savior had to deal with *BOTH* bondages in the same sacrifice—the shedding of His Life-blood— *TO SECURE* for us total-deliverance for our total-being. People's fallen-nature binds them to the devil *BY* their-disposition-to-sin. *Jesus liberated us from Satan's hold upon us by destroying our-old-disposition!* (John 12:31, 16:11, Colossians 1:13, Hebrews 2:14) In addition,...

There is a third area of separation from our lifestyle of the past—*THE MANY CURSES* that have been forced on mankind by that unholy-alliance between mankind and the devil. *One mistake many Christians make is to THINK they are resisting the devil, WHILE yielding their bodies, families and finances to the devil's destructive-works—curses resulting from Adam's-fall.* (John 10:10, 1 John 3:8) *The devil and his works are INSEPARABLE!* When sickness, poverty, fear, etc.—curses—attack us, the devil is surely involved. *Thus, resisting the curses is resisting the devil! His WORK is MORE than temptation to commit sin.* When Christ was on earth, *when He cast out demons, afflictions those evil-spirits had inflicted on the victims went with the demons.* (Matthew 4:24, 8:16, 9:33, 17:18) It still works the *SAME. The devil, Adam's fallen-nature and curses are intricately-linked-together.* Therefore, in His sacrifice, the Savior could not take on one of those three problems, and leave off either of the other two: It was all or nothing for both Christ and us. Jesus truly does save to the uttermost! (Hebrews 7:25)

Galatians 2:20: "I, [Paul, have been] crucified *WITH* Christ: Nevertheless, I live. Yet not I, but *Christ lives in me*: And, the life I now live in the flesh, *I LIVE BY THE FAITH OF THE SON OF GOD.*" That is the very heart of the Gospel. *TRUE-Christianity is based on FAITH in the sacrifice of Jesus Christ—His DEATH, His BURIAL and His RESURRECTION.* Any claims to salvation not based on Christ's sacrifice are *RELIGIOUS-FANTASIES!*

The life Christ came to impart to us may be enjoyed *ONLY* by True-New-Covenant-believers—*those who are born again and daily walk in fellowship with the Savior.* (John 10:9-10, Philippians 2:1, 1 John 1:2-3) *The only TWO OPTIONS available to us are*: Sticking with sinful-Adam, or trusting Jesus Christ—no mixture of the two.

In His one-sacrifice, *Jesus addressed every problem facing the human race—for all of time and eternity.* Had Jesus *LEFT INTACT* any portion of our predicament, as religion usually does, He would have helped nobody in any way. His only options were to address man's total-enslavement, *OR* leave the problems untouched. When Christ finished His redemptive-work, the devil was left in control of no one who is born-again and knows their rights in Christ. *The devil was CAST OUT.* (John 12:31) Thus, *he is an OUTCAST to people who know the truth about those New-Covenant-blessings, and walk in them by faith. Neither the devil nor his works have any legal-right to dominate believers! Only if he can talk believers into believing his lies can the devil bring destruction into their lives.* Thus, it is smart to be Bible-smart!

Since our Savior in His sacrifice NEGLECTED NOT to deal with every Adam-connected-problem; how may we escape if we NEGLECT the salvation our Lord provided? (Hebrews 2:3) A lot more than the-forgiveness-of-sins!

Ephesians 4:22-24: Believers are to *put off* (disrobe themselves of) *the old (corrupt-) man* and *put on* (clothe themselves with) *the new-man* (Christ). Colossians 3:9-10 says basically the same. *The old* (natural-)*man* (self) *is corrupt by its nature, so believers are to bring none of those old-corrupt-attributes into their new-life-in-Christ.* (Yet many do anyway!) *We identify with either ADAM or CHRIST—NEVER WITH BOTH AT THE SAME TIME!*

Galatians 6:14 also says that through Jesus Christ, *we believers have been crucified unto the world and the world unto us believers. The cross of Christ SEPARATES Christians from the world-system—which is crumbling.* (Daniel 7:9-14, 26-27, John 12:31, 1 Corinthians 2:6, 7:31, 1 John 2:17, Revelation 11:15) Also in Christ,...

ALL-OLD-things (of our-old-sinful-life) *have passed away.* (2 Corinthians 5:17) Our old-goals, motivations, purposes and relationships became drastically-altered: *We are brand-new on the inside.* And when one is born again, and begins that *NEW-LIFE* of fellowship with the Savior, he or she usually loses some *so-called-friends.* Paul wrote in 2 Corinthians 6:14-16 that believers and non-believers have little in common—opposites in fact. *Believers even become a separate-NATION!* (1 Peter 2:9) New-Covenant-believers and unbelievers have *different destinies*: (John 5:28-29) Such being because believers and unbelievers *SERVE* diametrically-opposed-*LORDS.* (1 John 5:18-19) One more separation-truth,...

Romans 6:9: Christ being raised from the dead, *He dies no more; for death has no more dominion over Him.* Verse-ten: He died unto sin *ONCE* (for all time—having solved all human-problems in that *ONE*-sacrifice): But in that He lives, He lives unto God (forever). What were the redemptive-results for us? Romans 6:11: "*Likewise* [because of Christ's-sacrifice], *consider yourselves also to be dead unto sin and alive unto God through Christ.*" When our Savior died to sin, we died to sin *WITH* Him: We *NOW* live to God *WITH* Him. *Death no longer having authority over our Resurrected-Savior, then neither does spiritual-death have dominion over believing-Christians. Neither does that old-sinful-self hold any power over us Christians. Our-old-man having died with Christ, we do not have to yield to old-habits, or relationships. We now being aligned with the Prince of Peace; we are no longer aligned with that liar and murderer!* (John 8:44)

Colossians 1:13 says God has (past-tense) delivered (rescued) us (believers) from the authority-of-darkness (the devil's-domain—Acts 26:18); *AND* has (past-tense) transferred us into the Kingdom of His dear Son. Thus, the devil is not lord over us new-creatures; because he is not lord over Christ—in Whom we reside! So, neither our former-evil-lifestyle nor Satan has any claim to our allegiance. *We DIED to BOTH through the-Lord's-death.* Remember that while Christ suffered on that cross, the Father looked on Him as the *Judged-Serpent* on a pole. (John 3:14) But when Christ *ROSE* from the dead, that old-Serpent was gone—the cursed-snake appeared not in the resurrected-Savior! Thus, we who are in Him are also *Serpent-free!* Ephesians 4:27 *commands believers to give NO PLACE to the devil—for God has given him no place in believers.* The devil can afflict believers only if they, *either in ignorance, or outright-rebellion,* open the door for his entrance. (John 17:15, 2 Corinthians 2:11, James 4:7, 1 Peter 5:8-9, 1 John 5:18) *Satan is on the outside, looking in; and cannot get in, unless we let him in.* Sadly, much of the church has let him in! Yet,...

Matthew 18:18 says: "Whatever you believers *BIND* [*forbid* to occur] upon earth will be *BOUND* [*forbidden*] by heaven: And whatever you [believers] *LOOSE* [*permit* to occur] on earth will be *LOOSED* [*permitted* to occur] by heaven." *Heaven backs our devil-resisting-actions!*

What most Christians have failed to grasp, however, *is that: WHEN our Savior delivered us from our-old-sin-nature, and from the devil himself, He ALSO set us free from all of the curses that came upon humanity through Satan and sin!* All three being CONNECTED, Christ had to *JUDICIALLY*-deal with all three of them on the cross. Thus, believers are not obligated to either of the three!

When Jesus emerged from the tomb He was totally-free from all three. *So when we identify with Christ, we enjoy the same-freedom from that evil-triplet.* Galatians 3:13 states: *"Christ HAS* [past-tense] *redeemed us from the curse of the law."* Making that a present-reality!

The Greek word rendered *REDEEMED* in Galatians 3:13 is *a commercial term meaning to buy up all there is to buy.* On the cross, Jesus bought every one of us and every part of each of us—leaving nothing untouched of all that evil had touched in our lives. And, since Christ purchased all of those things for us, all of those things belong to us! In that same-sacrifice, He also purchased us. So, we too belong to Christ! *We belong not to Satan, this world; or even to ourselves.* We are God's-property. (John 15:19, Acts 20:28, 1 Corinthians 6:19-20)

Deuteronomy 28:15-68 lists a multitude of *CURSES* that result from disobedience to God (sin). *God warned Israel that all those curses would PLAGUE them, if they refused to OBEY Him.* The curses affect people's spirit, soul, body, finances, property—and those who are dear to us. If curses prevail in one's life, it is either because of deliberate-sin, or ignorance-within, of the truth that Jesus saved us from those curses. (Galatians 3:13-14)

In either case, God is displeased with any suffering of any-such-evils. (Ezekiel 18:32) *Christ BORE all those cross-curses so that we would not have to BEAR them! Destruction-of-every-kind is Satan's-PLAN for mankind*; while "God is not willing that anybody perish." (2 Peter 3:9) Psalms 84:11: *"No good thing will God WITHHOLD from any who live uprightly."* John 10:10: *"Christ came, so that we might have ABUNDANT-LIFE."* Romans 8:32: *"God sparing not His own Son, but delivering Him up to the cross for us all—how will He not through Jesus also freely give us ALL THINGS that Jesus purchased for us on that cross?"* God is not a liar or thief! Therefore,...

Since both Father and Son were willing that the Son be sacrificed, then both must have WANTED us to enjoy the blessings provided by that sacrifice! So, how should God respond to people who refuse to believe and receive the blessings which cost both of them so very much???

ONLY Satan and religion would have us believe that the blessings Christ paid such an extreme-price for, so we could receive them during this-age, were actually for some-other-age—past or future—but NOT for Christians today. ONLY Satan and religion want us to believe that Christ becoming a curse on that cross was not enough to HEAL us today like it did in the church's early-days. According to MOST religious-traditions today, somehow, over time, Christ's shed-blood lost much of its power to save to the uttermost! (Hebrews 7:25) *NOT SO!!!*

When Jesus Christ rose from the dead, was He still partially-dead? Was He accompanied by even one sin? Did He still have symptoms of sickness clinging to His body? If so, then our being identified with Jesus Christ would mean we must suffer the same ourselves. But, *if our resurrected-Lord was and still is sin-free, sickness-free, poverty-free, failure-free and Serpent-free; then so are we!* Remind yourself often that: "As He [our Savior] is, so are we [even now] in this-world." (1 John 4:17)

Chapter Fourteen

Our brand-new-life-in-Christ

In light of the Bible-Truth that our Lord purchased our *complete-deliverance* from our *sinful-lifestyle,* from *Satan,* and from *all the curses* introduced to this earth by Adam's fall, *God obviously does NOT appreciate His NEW-creatures flirting with the-OLD-lifestyle, SATAN or any of THOSE CURSES!* Was that not Israel's downfall? Fresh out of Egypt, they murmured about returning to Egypt—which had become to Israel a *COMFORT-ZONE! They actually accused God and Moses of bringing upon them a worse-existence than they had suffered in their Egyptian-bondage—refusing to believe God's promise to Israel of a much-better-life in a* "land flowing with milk and honey." (Exodus 3:8, 17, Numbers 13:31-14:4) *As repayment for their unbelief, they roamed unnecessarily in the wilderness forty-long-years on an otherwise-few-week-journey.* Many Christians suffer similarly today!

God does not want New-Covenant-believers living in some kind of wilderness-existence; as the Israelites did. Bible-Christianity is not a no-man's-land. Just as with Israel, our *Lord RESCUED US* from a bondage-lifestyle; *NOT TO DEPRIVE US OF LIFE, BUT TO ELIMINATE OUR ODIOUS-PAST-LIFE*—which was actually killing us—*so that we may partake of GOD-LIFE even during this-age; and then look forward to heaven in the future.* God does not demand that believers wait for the *sweet-by-and-by* (heaven) *to enjoy the GOOD-LIFE!* In John 10:10, Jesus stated: "I came [to earth, so] that [believers] might have [zooee—God-]life; and have that [God-life] abundantly." And Jesus meant now during this-present-evil-age!

Christ's express-purpose for visiting the earth being to *GIVE LIFE* to mankind, and He having shown up for work, then He surely achieved that Godly-purpose—for according to Isaiah 55:11, *even the Lord Himself would not have been allowed to RETURN to heaven had He not completed the work His Father SENT Him to DO.* Thus, the very fact that Christ was received back into heaven *is proof that abundant-life has been available to people for around two-thousand-years. It is not physical-death that ushers us into LIFE, but DEATH to sin and the god-of-this-evil-age; AND our spiritual-rebirth into the family of God during this-evil-age!* And that means,...

Only those spiritually-united with Christ through the new-birth have the God-life Christ provided. Acts 4:12: *"For, there is salvation in NO other* [than Jesus Christ]: *There is NO OTHER NAME on earth, having been given among men, whereby we are to be saved."* The Word of God says that *our union with Christ in His death, burial and resurrection makes us partakers of that very same resurrection-life.* (John 14:19, Romans 6:3-5) God-life is inseparable from Christ's resurrection-life! Acts 9:2, 18:25, 19:9, 23, 22:4 call Christianity *THE WAY.* Thus, *Christianity is a LIFESTYLE; not just a religious-routine. God expects Christians today to have the SAME-FAITH-ATTITUDE AND SAME-FAITH-LIFESTYLE as Christians had in the early-church-days.* (Acts 5:20, Jude 3)

Deuteronomy 6:23 is an Old-Testament-Example of a New-Testament-Truth: *"God brought us OUT of Egypt to bring us INTO the land of Canaan."* God saved Israel from their former-Egyptian-lifestyle of extreme-poverty, crushing-disappointment and unending-misery, to give them freedom to worship Him in the land of unlimited-prosperity. *God wanted His people to possess the BEST of everything; AND to acknowledge that HE provided it!* (Deuteronomy 6:10-12, 8:7-20, 28:47-48) Therefore,...

If in yesteryear God wanted not His people to waste their precious-lives wandering in some uninhabitable-wilderness, *He does not want believers to do so TODAY!* Hebrews 11:40: *GOD PROVIDED SOME BETTER-THING FOR NEW-COVENANT-BELIEVERS THAN FOR ISRAEL!* New-Testament-Christians have *A BETTER-COVENANT* with *BETTER-PROMISES* than did Israel. (Hebrews 8:6) In fact, Romans 11:11 urges New-Testament-Inductees to live in such a way to *PROVOKE* the Jews to jealousy. Not many Christians have done that! We can, however, *if we start BELIEVING Gospel-Truth and PRACTICING it in our lives, rather than patronizing senseless-religious-traditions.* Jews will go for no message that *MINIMIZES* material, financial and physical-blessing—*emphasizing deliverance for the spirit ONLY—as most denominations do today.* God has retracted no New-Covenant-promise pertaining to any part of the human-constitution—and neither have theologians a right to do so. *Believe that!*

Genuine-Christians are intricately-connected to the *having-been-crucified-but-now-resurrected-Savior, Who rightly-expects us Christians to be totally-impacted and consistently-guided by that close-relationship with Him.* My old-sinful-self has been done away by my affiliation with Christ. *As far as GOD is concerned, that sinful-self exists no more; because He SEES me as a new-creature in Christ!* (2 Corinthians 5:17) Any *supposed-Christian-lifestyle* that comes short of Christ's resurrection-life is equivalent to Israel's wilderness-wanderings—tolerated by church-members either because of rebellion against God's revealed-will, or gross-ignorance of the blessings provided by God's Son on the cross. *Such tragedies are the result of the believer's personal-decisions—not some Divine-decree.* God provided in Christ the very best for Christians, *just as He did for Israel.* Heaven's-blessings are attached to Christ. *None exist outside of Him!*

So, this question will naturally arise: "If Christians are *NEW-CREATURES* in Christ, and *ALL OLD-THINGS HAVE PASSED AWAY, how can Christians commit sin?*" Answer: *It is one's spirit that gets born again, not one's old-mindset, or body!* As a spiritual-babe in Christ, the believer's new-born-spirit is usually *dominated by their old-way-of-thinking. Paul said we must be transformed by the renewing of our minds.* (Romans 12:2) And, Paul was writing to believers! *MOST new-converts carry with them a load of pre-Christian-baggage from their former-life.* Thus, *we have to reorient our mind and retrain our body—both of which are used to having their own way.* (1 Corinthians 3:1-4) *By nourishing our new-born-spirit through absorbing and practicing God's Word, our new-born-spirit will gradually mature* (1 Peter 2:2); *and start dominating every facet of our NEW-life* (Romans 12:1-2)—*our tripartite-being* (spirit, soul and body) *coming into proper-alignment with heavenly-purposes. AS WE MATURE SPIRITUALLY, WE WILL SIN LESS AND LESS!* (Hebrews 5:12-14) *That explains why,...*

Scripture DEMANDS that we subject our lifestyle and religious-doctrines to the SCRUTINY-of-Scripture. Within the religious-realm discrepancies abound; and worldly-wisdom is confusing at best. ANY lifestyle derived from either realm that does not line up with Scripture must be examined in the light of Scripture; and then restructured according to the unchanging-dictates of Scripture.

Ephesians 4:22-24 commands believers to *PUT OFF the-old-man* (self) *which is CORRUPT IN ALL ITS WAYS!* Also see Colossians 3:9-10. *We are to put off THE-OLD, AND put on THE-NEW.* Galatians 3:27 also informs us: "*As many of you as have been baptized into Christ have PUT ON Christ.*" *That actually means to clothe ourselves with Christ. If our being born again is putting on Christ, putting off the-old-man is our severance from Adam!*

In Scripture, there is no neutral-position—no middle-ground. The ONLY choices are life and death; according to Deuteronomy 30:19, John 3:18, 36, *ETC.* Moreover, The Lord said in John 15:5: "I am the Vine and you are the branches: He who abides in [union with] Me, and I in him, the same brings forth much fruit: For, without [severed from] Me you can produce no fruit at all." God sees every human being either *IN CHRIST* or *IN ADAM! God did not send Christ into the world just to SPURCE-UP our-old-sinful-self. He revolutionized our disposition, in order to upgrade our position!* (Hebrews 12:22-24)

The branch cannot produce fruit without nutrients supplied from the root through the vine. *No branch can even live without being connected to the vine!* However, neither may the root produce fruit without the branch, on which grows the fruit! *While we must be united with the Vine both to live and be productive, the Vine NEEDS us to stay in UNION with Him to fulfill His fruit-bearing-capabilities. And, God does EXPECT us to produce fruit!* (John 15:1-8) The devil does everything he can to stop believers from producing fruit—*either by attempting to PREVENT our union with Christ from forming in the first place—or TO SEVER that union, once it is formed.* (Mark 4:14-20) *The devil knows that he can no longer control people, who learn who they are in Christ, and take their stand on Bible-Truth. Victory over the devil requires that Christians come into, and remain in, union with Christ. The devil fears not our religious-routines—He does yield to the authority we have in Christ!* (James 4:7) Also,...

Romans 11:16: *"If the Root* [Jesus Christ] *is holy, so are the branches* [believers]." Thus, believers partake of the very holiness of the Vine—producing pure and holy fruit. The Savior supplies holy-sap, and new-creatures produce holy-fruit from it! (John 15:5) In addition,...

Jesus Christ stated in John 6:53 that *unless we eat His flesh and drink His blood WE HAVE NO LIFE IN US.* That is a *graphic-illustration* that drives home the point that only those who have an intimate-relationship with Jesus Christ (the Vine) partake of Divine-life. And,...

Ephesians 5:30: *"WE are members of HIS* [Christ's] *body, His flesh, and His bones."* Now that is as close to another person as one can get! Just as your limbs are part of your body, and your body is part of you, in the same manner, believers, made of spirit, soul and body, are a vital part of Christ on earth. Indeed, believers are the *ONLY* manifestation of Christ on earth! Also,...

"He who is joined to the Lord is one Spirit with Him." (1 Corinthians 6:17) So believers are not only members of Christ's Body (verse-fifteen); but are united with His Spirit as well. And not only the individual believer,...

For, Christ prayed in John 17:21: "That they all [all believers, from that day to this,] may *be ONE* [in unity]; *AS YOU* Father, are *IN ME*, and *I IN YOU*; *that they also MAY BE ONE* [unified] *IN US."* An intimacy neither this fallen-world nor the church-at-large understands! *God arranged for New-Covenant-believers to be one with the Son, the Father, and one another.* To achieve that,...

"God was in Christ, reconciling the world to Himself [while the Lord was on the cross]." (2 Corinthians 5:19) Moreover, 2 Peter 1:4 says that believers are at present "partakers of the *Divine-nature*—we having escaped the corruption which is in the world through lust." Neither of those passages leaves any room for some middle-of-the-road-existence for believers. Nor are new-creatures some mixture of the human and Divine! Because,...

"As He [Christ] is, so are we [believers] in this world [right now]." (1 John 4:17) Is our Savior in bondage to sin? Is He sick? Is He confused? Is Jesus broke, or just barely getting by these days? Is our Lord discouraged?

No again and again! Well, if none of those problems belong to Jesus Christ our Savior, then neither do they belong to knowledgeable and obedient-Christians. Our settling for anything less than what He wrought for us on the cross cheats us out of many of the blessings He wrought for us on the cross! Of course, the words: "As He is, so are we in-this-world," apply to the Christian's reborn-spirit, and not directly to our flesh. But, we are to live our Christian-life from that spiritual-connection to Christ; *which enables us to overcome flesh-problems too!* "By His wound we are healed," etc., etc., etc.

The Gospel is filled with many blessings, which only active, consistent, faithful-believers will receive. Divine-benefits do not automatically accompany any Christian! We must do OUR part to receive the purchased-benefits: OUR part is to OBEY the Benefit-Provider. By increasing both our faith-and-obedience-levels, the Gospel-benefits WILL CHASE US DOWN MORE FREQUENTLY. The first few chapters of Acts recorded how thoroughly-changed were the lives of the first-century-Christians. ALL their NEEDS were met—They were well-fed, received healing in their bodies, and were full of joy. Believers did suffer persecution, however, because persecution comes with the Christian-life-package. But, they were triumphant, even in the midst of persecution! Now this truth,...

Neither the devil, the world-system, nor religion can stand the thought of anyone succeeding in life without using their ideas, goods or services; *so they PRESSURE Christians to fall back under their EVIL-regimes through compromise. The devil, the unsaved, and that religious-*

bunch ATTEMPT TO CONTROL OTHERS when they can. To obtain that manipulative-control, they CONTEND that only they can meet our every need: ONLY their brand of automobile, credit-card, pain-reliever and TOOTHPASTE will make us happy. Moreover, *joining the JUST-RIGHT-CHURCH-DENOMINATION IS THE VERY CAPSTONE OF THE-RELIGIOUS-ONE'S LIFE. The devil uses this world-system and religion to promote his demonic-agenda! So believers need to learn the Bible-Truth that EVERY ONE of our needs is ultimately-met through Christ's sacrifice; including protection from demonic-deception, the world-system and religion.* Bow not before either of them!

The sections of this book dealing with the problems of human-identification have generally been longer and more involved than the ones presenting *THE ANSWER-SIDE*. That is no accident or oversight. In Deuteronomy twenty-eight, the first-fourteen-verses list the blessings of the Mosaic-law—*promised to the obedient-patrons of that Mosaic-law—the rest of that chapter* (verses 15-68) *detailing many terrible curses people would experience if they disobeyed the commands of that law.* Thus,...

SIN COMPLICATES life; while obedience *SIMPLIFIES* everything in life. *Disobedience multiplied Eve's sorrow and conception. But, Adam fared no better. Because of his disobedience, he would sweat for his daily-bread all the rest of his life. Adam and Eve left the SIMPLICITY of plucking and eating in their garden-paradise; to labor in the fields, cook their meals, clean up afterwards, and to suffer indigestion to boot.* Conversely, our believing the Gospel-message simplifies our lives. So, let us learn all we can about it! This book is a good starting place!

The next chapter goes into detail about some of the blessings, which belong to us through our relationship with that One Whom the Father brought back from the dead, and made both Lord and Christ. (Acts 2:36)

Chapter Fifteen

All things are ours in Christ!

ALL THINGS HAVE BECOME NEW TO EVERYBODY IN CHRIST. (2 Corinthians 5:17) *And, those new-things are ALL OF GOD—none are of our-old-life, of the world-system, or of the devil.* As far as God is concerned, that old-sinful-lifestyle no longer exists. *God looks upon us through Christ and the cross.* Because our Savior died, was buried, and then made alive again, people who are *IN* (have been joined unto) Jesus Christ partake of the same-spiritual-conditions! (John 5:24) Our evil-nature passed away by virtue of our union with our Lord; and a new-creation has taken its place. So in every respect, God expects us to experience that new-life. In fact, God *COMMANDS* all of us who are in Christ to both live and minister as Christ lived and ministered! (1 John 2:6)

What do we do with people who have passed away? *We bury them!* Now, I mean no disrespect for the dead: I only point out the truth that we separate dead-things from ourselves. We put decaying-stuff out of our sight. Water-baptism symbolizes our burial of that old-sinful-being—*God raising us up to a brand-new-life in Christ.* How much of that corpse do we bury? The entire body! Why is it necessary to put the entire-dead-body six feet under? Because, corpses are not only useless, they are even dangerous. They may serve as breeding-places for deadly-germs that could infect the living with sickness; bringing about more death. For that *REASON* alone, no matter how *CLOSE* we are to our loved-ones while they are alive, or how much we sorrow over their departure, we manage to overcome our grief and our reluctance to let them go by planting their body. *Another incentive is to hide the indignity decay inflicts upon the flesh of our loved-one by putting it in a fancy-casket in the ground.*

Well, if the urgency to prevent the spread of disease in the natural-realm overcomes that powerful-desire to cling to the corpse of the one we love, *why do so many believers TENACIOUSLY hold onto that old-body-of-sin? "That old-sinful-self has been crucified with Christ, that the body-of-sin might be rendered totally-ineffective; so that we should not serve sin."* (Romans 6:6) But, *many church-members are bound by their past. They will not let it go; either in their mindset, or lifestyle!* However, in order to enter that new-life Jesus Christ won for us on the cross, we must sever all connections to our sin and curse-ridden-*PAST-LIFE.* (1 Corinthians 1:18-31, 3:18) One New-Testament-negative-example:

Jesus Christ described certain Christians as being *wretched and miserable and poor and blind and naked.* (Revelation 3:17) *How could those conditions possibly be God's will for the redeemed? Redemption solved both the sin-problem and the curse-problem of our old-life*—why Christ redeemed us! Also, consider this obviously-little-known-to-most-of-the-church-Bible-Truth:

Had God wanted sinners to remain sinners, *BUT* be blessed anyway, He would not have expelled Adam and Eve from that Garden-Paradise despite their treason. *If the Creator had granted those two access to that tree of life while in their sinner-state, they would have forever existed as criminals; growing ever-more-vile as the ages rolled by.* (Genesis 3:22-24) *A BIG WHY of redemption!*

Did God alter His creation and salvation-plans when modern-times fell upon us? Would He allow us today to get by with something He would not permit in the lives of Adam and Eve? Actually, believers today will be held even more accountable than they, because we can look back on history and see the *awful consequences of sin*. WE have God's-Written-Word, the Bible, which exposes the deceptiveness and destructiveness of sin. To whom more has been given, of that one more will be required; and that truth is just as true in our dealings with God, as it is with men. (Luke 12:47-48, Acts 17:30, Romans 1:20, 2:1, 1 Corinthians 10:11, James 4:17) Thus,...

We Christians are expected to forsake and forget our sinful-past—then press toward the mark for the prize of the HIGH-calling of God in Christ. (Philippians 3:13-14) Psalms 45:10-11: "Hearken, daughter [Christians], and consider; incline your ear. *Forget also your-own-people and your-father's-house* [all your past]: *So will the King greatly desire your beauty; for He* [Jesus Christ] *is your Lord; and worship Him.*" God having raised us up with His Son (Ephesians 2:6), we are commanded to set our affection on things that are above; not on things on the earth. (Colossians 3:1-2) And, to: "*Love not this world, nor the things that are in this world.*" (1 John 2:15-17)

What *MANY* people cherish deteriorates before their very eyes: (2 Corinthians 4:18, James 4:13-14) Which is why God forbids our chasing after *temporal-stuff.* He made us human beings for higher, eternal-purposes.

Galatians 3:13 *tells us that through what Christ did on the cross, WE WERE REDEEMED FROM THE CURSE OF THE LAW.* (Deuteronomy 28:15-68) And the *CURSE* included all sickness and poverty. Verse-fourteen tells why Christ rescued us from that terrible-fate: *That the blessing of Abraham might come upon Gentile believers through Jesus Christ. No middle-ground is mentioned in this or any other Scripture passage. God's Word clearly teaches that EITHER curses OR blessings will dominate our life!* (Deuteronomy 28:1-14, 15-68) *That Greek term rendered redeemed in* Galatians 3:13 *means to buy up all there is to buy—Which means Christ purchased our complete-redemption from every form and degree of the curses of Moses' law—ALL PAINFUL AND DEGRADING-CONDITIONS.* (Deuteronomy 28:15-68) In contrast,...

Check out Abraham's blessings: *"Abraham was old and well-stricken-with-age: But the Lord had BLESSED Abraham IN ALL THINGS: silver, gold, cattle!"* (Genesis 13:2, 17:1-8, 24:1) So, being *BLESSED IN ALL THINGS* was a vital-part of the Abrahamic-Covenant. How does that covenant God made with Abraham *AND* his *SEED* 3500 years ago affect us believers today? Paul wrote in Galatians 3:16, 29 *that ALL of the PROMISES made to Abraham were ALSO made to his SEED* (Jesus Christ); *and that we, who are IN CHRIST, are Abraham's-Seed.* So, God's promises to Abraham are for believers today! And, the redemptive-blessings Christ purchased for us through His cross-sacrifice are the same blessings God blessed Abraham *AND* his Seed with in ancient-times! Deuteronomy 28:15-68 reveals the curses as sickness, poverty, fear, bondage; and a whole lot more. Blessings being the very opposite of curses, and our Lord having removed the curses from us (by becoming accursed in our place), all that He bought for us on the cross have to be Abraham's blessings—including health, material and financial-prosperity, intact families, success in all of our endeavors, and a whole-lot-more. (Luke 1:68-73, 13:16, Romans 4:13, Galatians 3:9, 13-14) Because,...

God did not grant Abraham just a few-perks in life. He promised the man *ALL-blessings*—and his heirs the very same! Am I overstating the case? Jesus was called the *SEED* of Abraham in Galatians 3:16; and WE WHO ARE IN CHRIST by our new-birth are inside that *SEED*. (1 Corinthians 12:12-13, Galatians 3:26-29) Thus,...

Whatever Jesus purchased at Calvary belongs to us who believe—because our Savior needed none of those components of salvation for Himself. What He achieved on the cross was placed in the account of all of us who believe upon and confess Christ as our Savior and Lord! (Romans 6:6-11, 10:9-10, 17) More Bible-evidence,...

All the promises of God in Christ are yes and amen: To the glory of God by Christians receiving them! None of His promises are maybe or maybe-not. *Our believing for and receiving the promised-blessings is what brings glory to God!* (2 Corinthians 1:20) *Any DECISION to not believe for and receive those blessings OFFENDS God!*

Ephesians 1:3 says God has (past-tense) blessed us believers with all-spiritual-blessings in heavenly-places in Christ. How many? *ALL!* Where? *IN CHRIST! And we Christians are IN CHRIST!* The blessings being spiritual does not restrict them to our *SPIRIT*; or mean they may be enjoyed only after our physical-death. The blessings are spiritual because God, Who is Spirit, is the Source. *They are meant to manifest in the natural-realm during the-present-age; and some of course, up in heaven both now and later. Spiritual-blessings on the INSIDE sooner or later affect circumstances on the OUTSIDE!* (Proverbs 4:20-22, 14:30, 17:22, 18:14, 22:4) Bible-proof,...

Faith is a *spiritual-substance*, according to Hebrews 11:1. *The faith-hall-of-fame* (Hebrews 11:1-40) *recounts the many different ways the spiritual-substance of faith manifested itself in the natural-realm in the lives of Old-Covenant-Saints.* And, *every instance of bodily-healing, provision and deliverance our Lord ministered to people in His earth-ministry was by that spiritual-substance of faith. Our Lord ministered to folks by Holy-Spirit-power* (Matthew 12:28, Luke 4:18) *in response to their FAITH; and SPOKE Spirit-Words* (Matthew 8:8, John 6:63) *that affected people's sick-bodies; AND other circumstances*: Christ multiplied food, killed a fruitless-fig-tree, turned water into wine, healed every kind of sickness, calmed windstorms and even walked on water *by the spiritual-substance of faith; and then commanded believers to do those same kinds of things.* (Matthew 17:20, 18:18-20, 21:22, Mark 16:15-18, Luke 6:40, John 14:12-14, Acts 1:1, 8, James 5:14-16) How was that made possible?

God Who spared not His own Son (the sufferings of the cross), but delivered Him up to the cross for us all, will with Him also freely give us all things which Christ purchased for us on the cross: (Romans 8:32) *Meaning that everything our Savior wrought on the cross belongs to ALL of us who believe the Gospel-message.* Extent of the blessings promised to Abraham and his Seed:

"*The promise that he would become heir of the world was not to Abraham or to his Seed through the Mosaic-law, but by the righteousness of FAITH.*" (Romans 4:13) *Proving that not just a few-barely-get-by-blessings, but the WORLD itself, was included in God's promise to that man of faith—and to everyone who will follow his faith-example.* Now tying some passages together,...

Hebrews 1:2: God *HAS* in these-last-days spoken to us by His Son (Jesus); *Whom He HAS appointed heir of all things.* All things would certainly include this world. Galatians 3:29 *says that we New-Covenant-Christians are the Seed of Abraham through our union with Christ; so we are heirs of the world and everything in it just as much as Abraham and Christ are!* Romans 8:17 agrees that *we Christians are heirs of God and joint-heirs with Christ* (Abraham's-Seed). We have a rich-inheritance!

The Savior Himself said that the New Covenant was *IN HIS BLOOD* (Luke 22:20); *which He deposited on the heavenly-altar* (Hebrews 9:12)—*where NO moth, rust or thief may pollute it or destroy it.* (Matthew 6:19-20) *And so; no New-Covenant-blessing bought by Christ's blood shed on the cross has been deleted from that blood. Nor has the power of that blood deteriorated since our Lord deposited it on that altar in heaven. All are still INTACT, and still AVAILABLE to all who believe the Gospel!*

Only three-categories of blessings are now available to humanity: Blessings of *original-creation* (which were contaminated by Adam's sin)—the blessings under the *Mosaic-Covenant*; and those in the *resurrected-Christ— New-Testament-blessings. And, there are three-types of human beings that need blessings—Jews, Gentiles and the Church.* (1 Corinthians 10:32, Ephesians 2:11-18, Colossians 1:21) Yet, *even the Old-Covenant-Blessings enjoyed by many JEWS over many centuries had to be paid for by the blood-sacrifice of the promised-Messiah.* Romans 3:25 and Hebrews 9:15 prove that sins under the Old Covenant had not been cancelled; just covered. Only the blood of Christ could actually *REMOVE* them. *Unsaved-humans have ONLY nature's-TAINTED-bounty to look forward to* (Matthew 6:32); while Christians can enjoy both the goodies in nature and those in Christ.

MAN is basically a spirit, possessing a soul, living in a body. Because man's fall affected every-aspect of his being, Jesus Christ addressed every-human-problem in His sacrifice: Our Savior paid the full-price to purchase benefits for spirit, soul, and body—sparing no expense, and shunning no area of human need.

Of course, *man's sinful-nature being man's primary- predicament, Christ tackled that monster right up front: Bearing the full-penalty for the sins of this entire-world; potentially delivering everyone from eternal-destruction.* (Isaiah 53:1-12, John 1:29, 3:16, 2 Corinthians 5:21, Hebrews 1:3, 9:23, 10:12, 1 John 2:2, Revelation 1:5)

So, in Christ we are free from both the *POWER* and *PENALTY* of our past-sins. However, redemption has to be believed and received! People who *REFUSE* to accept freedom from *SIN'S PENALTY AND POWER* during this-lifetime by heeding the Gospel, remain enslaved to sin, and will die in their sins, and bear sin's penalty for all eternity. (John 3:18, 36, 8:24) And that means,...

"*NOW* is the accepted-time: And, *NOW* is the day of salvation." (2 Corinthians 6:2) *Salvation is ours for the taking—but has to be received WHILE we are still alive. And, Godliness is PROFITABLE in this-life and the next.* (1 Timothy 4:8) So, *we do not have to wait until we die and go to heaven to enjoy that new-life-in-Christ.*

Our Lord redeemed us from sin (Romans 6:6), from the devil (Hebrews 2:14), and this world-system. (John 17:14, Galatians 1:4) Satan being the god of this world (2 Corinthians 4:4), and Christ having rescued us from this world (Galatians 1:4), then Satan is no longer our god! *When Jesus removed our sins, the devil lost control over all of us, whose sins have been removed! Our Lord delivered us from the authority-of-darkness—the devil's illegal-dominion.* (Acts 26:18, Colossians 1:13) Thus,...

Knowledgeable and obedient-believers may actually dominate the devil! When God raised our Lord from the dead, He enthroned Jesus at His right hand—far above *ALL principality, power, might* and *dominion; and above every name that is named*, in heaven and on the earth. (Ephesians 1:19-23) *The devil is surely on that list!* And Ephesians 2:6 says that we believers have been raised up with Christ and enthroned along with Him at God's right hand. So, believers have the same authority over the devil our Lord has! (John 8:31-32, Romans 16:20, Ephesians 4:27, James 4:7, 1 Peter 5:8-9) Moreover,...

If both Satan and sin have lost their power over us, then all of those curses resulting from sin and Satan's interference in our lives have lost their ability to afflict us as well! Deuteronomy 28:15-68 lists every suffering imaginable: sickness, financial-disaster, dysfunctional-families, failure at one's every undertaking, worry, war, captivity, traumatic death! No tragedy is excluded from that list. *BUT*, Galatians 3:13 says believers have been redeemed from all of the curses of the law, as recorded in that Deuteronomy-passage. So those curses have no more legal-power over believers than Satan or sin has!

Isaiah 53:4-5, 10, Matthew 8:16-17, Hebrews 13:8, and 1 Peter 2:24 *ALL teach that supernatural-healing is a permanent-blessing, belonging to the church of Jesus Christ to the end of this-age.* But, *supernatural-healing does not automatically manifest in a believer's life, any more than any other New-Testament-benefit. Receiving covenant-provisions is conditional on our personal-faith that THE SACRIFICE our Savior made on that cross was sufficient to BUY those provisions for us—along with our bold-confession that God is faithful to grant them.* Faith for what God has *BOTH* promised and provided comes by *HEARING* what God says about our needs, and His promises and provisions: (Romans 10:17) *NOT through powerless-religious-tradition.* (2 Timothy 3:5) According to God's Word, *all who are in Christ are healed already!* (1 Peter 2:24) *And that PART of the Gospel-provision is just as valid today as are all the other Gospel-PARTS.*

Isaiah 53:12 and 2 Corinthians 8:9 *declare that our Lord became poor to deliver us from poverty!* Religious-patrons will scream that such-statements cheapen the sacrifice that Jesus made—for they think that only our sins were worthy of such an extreme-price. But, since all those curses resulted from sin, and poverty was one of those curses, how could our Savior redeem us from our sin, without at the same time delivering us from all the results of our sin? Those religious-adherents make no claim that we must go to Hell, after receiving Christ as Savior, although Hell is one of sin's-many-penalties! Since God requires not that faithful-Christians burn in Hades, why would He want us to bear the other curses resulting from those sins; for which He forgave us? No one is authorized to draft his own religious-rules about that redemption-plan. *Christ redeemed us from EVERY FACET of the CURSE!* (Galatians 3:13) Think now,...

If Jesus Christ becoming sin with my sins *made me righteous* with His righteousness (2 Corinthians 5:21); and if His bearing my diseases *healed my body* (Isaiah 53:4-5, 10, Matthew 8:17, 1 Peter 2:24), then my Lord becoming poor with my poverty *has also made me rich.* (2 Corinthians 8:9) If I can experience any of the other cross-purchases during this-lifetime, I can surely have financial-prosperity; even as a believer. (Psalms 35:27, 2 Corinthians 8:9, 3 John 2) And not only that,...

Deuteronomy twenty-eight records additional facets of that curse, beside those we have dealt with already. And, Christ rescued us from *ALL* those facets as well—*providing redemption for our entire-being—replacing all of those curses with New-Covenant-blessings.*

Next we will see how NOT to gain the life-enhancing, redemptive-goodies Christ wrought for us on that cross. Furthermore, *neither those blessings, nor the receiving-process is for lazy-folks*: Those cross-blessings may be gained *ONLY* by fighting that *"GOOD FIGHT OF FAITH."* (1 Timothy 6:12, 2 Timothy 4:7) Need-to-know-stuff!

Chapter Sixteen

Improper-view of the how-to

The *BIG*-question asked by those who are desperate for relief is: *HOW? HOW may I be saved?* On the day of Pentecost, people under Holy-Spirit-conviction through Peter's message asked him that question: "What must we do to be saved [*from our miserable-condition*]?" (Acts 2:37) One rich young man asked the same of the Lord: "A certain ruler asked Jesus: 'Good Master, what must I [myself] do to inherit eternal life?'" (Luke 18:18) *Each of those salvation-seekers realized that there was some personal-responsibility connected with their redemption. Not one redemptive-blessing comes to us automatically.* Redemptive-promises remain unfulfilled until someone taps into them by faith, and obedience. *God fulfills HIS promises to people who meet HIS conditions.* "*You have need of patience; so that after you have done the will of God you will receive the promise.*" (Hebrews 10:36) God does not operate irresponsibly—*He blesses only people who believe in and obey His Word!* (James 1:22-25)

Many people disdain God's answer to their inquiry. That young ruler walked away *empty-hearted*, because the Lord's demand seemed unreasonable unto him. *He likely expected the Savior to recommend something his Jewish-teachers had overlooked in their instructions to him in his upbringing.* But, that was not the case. After hearing Christ's answer, instead of inquiring further of the Master, he just walked away, apparently assuming either that salvation for somebody like him was totally-off-limits, or that Jesus Christ was a fraud, or that the young preacher Himself was just-a-little-off-balance.

The young man evidently had a *preconceived-notion* that Jesus would suggest *he ADD some new-activity* to his observance of the Ten Commandments. *In addition to the more-than-six-hundred-laws the religious-leaders had LAID ON the general-Jewish-population, the young man probably figured he could tolerate one or two more religious-rules.* However, Jesus knew what was in man (John 2:25), so He went right to the heart of the matter by pointing out that young man's misplaced-trust. The ruler was putting his confidence in riches, rather than in God, Who provided riches. The Jews put great stock in passages like Deuteronomy 8:18—which taught that *God gave them power to get wealth.* Obviously, being a leader in the Jewish-economy, the young-dignitary was likely familiar with that Scripture; *but was reluctant to forgo his opulent-lifestyle to better acquaint himself with Him Who had made him rich in the first place.* The man learned the hard way that money makes a poor-god!

That man, like most folks today, obviously believed that salvation is something *added to one's current-life*; without demanding significant-changes in it. Although people admit they could use a little help, they desire to control that salvation-process. If a preacher gives them an answer they do not want to hear, they just make up their own rules about it—or start looking for a different church—whichever seems to require the least effort on their part. *SOME* even go start another church. That is how some denominations were formed. Yet, to be fair, I will admit that some people *HAVE TO GO ELSEWHERE* to obey God, and avoid compromising on His Word.

On that Day of Pentecost, however, those salvation-seekers responded differently. They neither contended with that preacher, nor sought a more tolerant church; but obeyed Peter's instructions (Acts 2:41-42)—*proving that there are people who are willing to obey God rather than argue with Him.* On the other hand, *there are both sinners and religious-folks, who will twist the simplest-Bible-instructions TO THE DESTRUCTION of themselves and others* (Matthew 22:29, Mark 7:13, 2 Peter 3:16)

ONE SUCH PERVERSION *is the misrepresentation of Peter's answer to the Pentecost-Day-Salvation-Seekers.* Theologians have converted Peter's words in Acts 2:38 into a religious-system pushing a slanted-view of *HOW PEOPLE GET BORN AGAIN.* That *GROSS-misconception* and *misapplication* of that passage has caused untold-confusion within the Body of Christ for two-centuries. My recent book: "The Cult That Calls Itself The Church Of Christ" *EXPOSES* that and other Church-Of-Christ-*ERRORS—NOT A FEW.* Nevertheless,...

My purpose is not so much to point out theological-error, as it is to discover *Bible-Truth* that makes people free. (John 8:31-32) However, *honest-research of Bible-Truth on any subject will reveal doctrinal-errors that are initiated by people with either GOOD or EVIL intentions.* Yet, whether intentional or unintentional, good or evil, the result of erroneous-teaching is always destructive! (2 Peter 3:16) Now investigating that gross-error,...

Acts 2:38: Peter instructed those who had *ASKED*: "What must we do?" "*Repent and be baptized every one of you in the name of Jesus Christ, for the remission of sins, and you will receive the gift of the Holy Spirit.*"

Religious-error will LIE UNDETECTED, until someone studies to find out what the Bible actually says about it; and then exposes the religious-error. Church-Of-Christ-preachers have wrung from that verse and a few others that immersion of the body in water is necessary for the soul-salvation of the one being put under water. But,...

In my research I have found more than three-dozen Scripture passages that reveal otherwise. *I suggest not that water-baptism has NO significance in the life of the believer—but I do point out that the Bible-significance is opposite that Church-Of-Christ-doctrine.* Notice,...

John 3:3-8: Nicodemus the Pharisee came to Jesus one night with a quizzical-mind and a searching-heart. That man did not realize what his *REAL*-problem was, but Christ knew just what he needed; and returned an answer that took him totally-off-guard. *A preconceived-religious-mindset blinded Nicodemus to the significance of Christ's response.* Jesus agreed not with Nicodemus; nor argued with him—but exposed the limitation of his mindset. *Christ did comment that it was Israel's great-misfortune to have such dense-religious-leaders—blind-leaders attempting to LEAD blind-followers.* (Luke 6:39) John 3:9-12 finishes that narrative.

Church-Of-Christ-theologians distort Christ's words in John 3:5 *to back their denominational-SLANT on the Gospel-message. They contend that Jesus Christ taught there that water-baptism is an absolute-necessity in the salvation-process.* Did He really teach that? First of all, the Greek-word for *baptism* does not appear anywhere in that entire-passage. *The Lord did mention water, but NOT of being immersed in water for salvation!* When He informed Nicodemus that he must be born again (from above), the man's thinking was restricted to the idea of natural-childbirth. *So that is what Jesus responded to!* To Nicodemus, another-birth meant *climbing back into his mother's womb to be born a second-time.* But Jesus instructed the Pharisee that a person must experience a *different-kind-of-birth—one taking place on the inside of the person—spiritual-rebirth originating from above—* not a second-natural-birth. Actual-Bible-Truth,...

The water our Lord spoke of in John 3:5 referred to *natural-childbirth! WHEN* a pregnant-woman's *WATER* breaks, her child will soon be born. *Spiritual-rebirth*, to the contrary, takes place in one's spirit by Holy-Spirit-activity! The Lord was clearly teaching that one has to experience a birth *IN BOTH REALMS*, in order to enter the Kingdom of God. Jesus certainly did not teach that one's spirit is reborn by immersing one's physical-body in *H2O. If a person has not been physically-conceived, so never physically-existed, he or she will obviously not be qualified for a spiritual-rebirth!* The Savior explained in John 3:6: "What is born of the flesh [water] is flesh; and what is born of the Spirit is spirit." Thus, we must admit that Christ's words in John 3:5 described *TWO-DIFFERENT-KINDS-OF-BIRTH; not two-realms involved in the rebirth of the spirit.* If Church-Of-Christ-theology *WERE* correct, then John 3:6 would make *NO SENSE! The Savior made it clear that He was speaking of births in two-different-realms: He was not teaching that water is part of the new-birth. We are not born FROM ABOVE by a combination of Holy-Spirit-activity ON OUR INSIDE and immersion of our body in water ON THE OUTSIDE. The new-birth is solely an inside-job by the Holy Spirit!*

Furthermore, if water-baptism bore the significance in Peter's day it is given by the Church Of Christ now, then why did Peter *NOT* emphasize immersion in water for one's salvation in other passages? In Acts 3:19, one chapter later, *Peter instructed another group of people how to get saved—without mentioning water-baptism at all:* "Repent, and be converted [their spiritual-response on the inside], that your sins may be blotted out." Acts 4:4 reports their joyful-response: "Many who heard the Word [Peter had just been preaching] believed: And the number came to be about five thousand." Did Peter or Luke (the author of Acts) mention those believers being water-baptized in that passage? I am sure they did get water-baptized—*but that is not emphasized*. Must all of Scripture be understood in the light of Acts 2:38 alone; or ought Acts 2:38 be understood in the light of all the rest of Scripture? And now check this out,...

Acts chapter-ten reports the conversion of a Roman centurion, named Cornelius, and a house-full of family and friends. Now, if one cannot be saved without being water-baptized, how did all those people get born again *BEFORE* they were water-baptized? "While Peter spoke those words, the Holy Spirit fell upon those who heard his words." (Acts 10:44) And Peter asked: "Can anyone forbid water, so that these should not be baptized, who have *RECEIVED* the Holy Spirit just as we have?" (Acts 10:47) *Can the unsaved RECEIVE the Holy Spirit? John 14:17 says unsaved-people CANNOT RECEIVE the Holy Spirit! The lost can ONLY be Holy-Spirit-convicted of sin, of righteousness, and of judgment.* (John 16:8-11) *But, Cornelius and his guests became BELIEVERS and were Holy-Spirit-baptized BEFORE they got water-baptized!*

Peter was accosted by a council of narrow-minded-Jewish-Christians about his unprecedented-activity at that Gentile's house—then Peter answered: "As I began to speak, the Holy Spirit fell on [those Gentile-believers just] as He did upon us at the beginning." (Acts 11:15) Peter referred to Pentecost, *WHEN* the Holy Spirit *FELL ON* that hundred-twenty. (*And no Scripture implies that the hundred-twenty in the upper room on that day were baptized in water, either before or after the resurrection of Christ!* Neither does the record show such occurred on that day of Pentecost. *If water-baptism had been as important then as many contend today, Scripture would surely have recorded the event!*) On one other occasion Peter had to defend his ministry at the Gentile's house:

In Acts 15:8-9, he assured those Christians of Jewish-ancestry that: "God Who *KNOWS* the hearts [of people], bore them [Cornelius and friends] witness; giving them the Holy Spirit *EVEN AS* He did unto us [at Pentecost]: And put no difference between us and them—*purifying their hearts BY FAITH [NOT by water-baptism]." Spirits do not get PURIFIED by water or ceremony.* Now this,...

Acts 9:17-18 says Ananias entered the house where Saul-of-Tarsus had been directed to stay; then put his hands on Saul, and said: "Brother Saul, the Lord, even Jesus, Who appeared to you on your way has sent me, that you might receive your sight, *and be filled with the Holy Spirit.*" Remember, the lost CANNOT RECEIVE the Holy Spirit (John 14:17)—*indicating that Saul was born again sometime during those three days. "Immediately, there fell from Saul's eyes something like scales; and he received his eye-sight.* Then Saul was baptized in water [AFTER being bodily-healed, and filled with the Spirit]." Bashing the Church-Of-Christ-water-baptism-heresy.

Acts 22:16 might at first *SEEM* to back that *water-baptism-falsehood*: Paul remembered that Ananias had said to him: "Why do you tarry? [What are you waiting for?] *Arise and be baptized AND wash away your sins; calling on the name of the Lord."* Saul was told both to be baptized, *AND to wash away his sins, calling on the name of the Lord. It is calling on the name of Jesus that washes away sins—not water-baptism!* Saul obviously was already saved to qualify for the infilling of the Holy Spirit. *THUS, washing away his sins was equivalent to Abraham sealing his faith with circumcision, after being declared righteous BY FAITH.* Acts 2:21 is Peter's quote of Joel 2:32: *"In the last-days, whosoever calls on the name of the Lord will are saved." There is no mention of water-baptism being involved; either by Joel or Peter.*

Did Peter fail to follow that water-baptism-doctrine, which he himself *supposedly-established* in Acts 2:38? Moreover, Paul quoted that same passage from Joel in Romans 10:13: "Whoever calls on the name of the Lord will be saved." *Neither Peter nor Paul taught that water-baptism must occur BEFORE one is born again!*

If water-baptism is what saves the lost, Paul helped few folks get saved in his ministry—because, he said in 1 Corinthians 1:17: *"Christ sent me NOT to baptize, but to preach the Gospel."* In Romans 1:16, Paul wrote that *the Gospel of Christ is the power of God to salvation for everyone who believes that Gospel. There is no mention of water-baptism in that passage either.* The run-away-slave, Onesimus, *got born again* under Paul's ministry; WHILE Paul was in prison in Rome! If water-baptism is essential to salvation, then, according to Philemon 10, the soldier guarding Paul must have sneaked a *TUB* of water into jail, to baptize Onesimus in; for Paul said he had *begotten* Onesimus in his imprisonment—his two-year-house-arrest in Rome. *That soldier responsible for Paul would not have allowed him to take Onesimus out of confinement to some body of water to baptize him!*

Romans 10:9-10 tells how one is saved; *and water-baptism is nowhere mentioned in that passage!* "If you CONFESS WITH YOUR MOUTH the Lord Jesus [as your Savior], AND BELIEVE IN YOUR HEART that God raised Him from the dead, you will be saved." Moreover,...

Not every occurrence of the word *BAPTISM* refers to water-baptism! In Luke 12:50, our Savior said: *"I have a baptism TO BE baptized with."* John the Baptizer had BAPTIZED JESUS WITH WATER at the beginning of His ministry—so what baptism did the Lord refer to in that verse? *The baptism of SUFFERING! Yet another baptism is that of FIRE!* (Luke 3:16) Fire and water being totally opposite, then fire-baptism has to be totally opposite of water-baptism. Another is the *transfer* that takes place in both spirit and body of people believing on Christ as their Savior. *"BY ONE SPIRIT WE BELIEVERS ARE ALL BAPTIZED INTO ONE BODY."* (1 Corinthians 12:13) So, *people are baptized INTO Christ BY Holy-Spirit-activity in their spirit; not BY the preacher immersing their body in water. Christians' bodies are members of Christ TOO!* (1 Corinthians 6:15) Yet, *water saves no one in either spirit or body. It is the work of the Holy Spirit ALONE!*

Every-kind-of-baptism involves three-elements: *One performing that baptism, the candidate being baptized, and the substance into which the candidate is baptized.* In water-baptism, *ministers DO the baptizing, believers GET baptized and WATER is the substance in which the believer is baptized.* In 1 Corinthians 12:13, *THE HOLY SPIRIT* does the baptizing, the *BELIEVER* gets baptized, and *THE BODY OF CHRIST* is the substance into which the believer gets baptized. Water is not involved! Christians are then baptized with the *HOLY SPIRIT.* (Matthew 3:11) *There are five different substances into which one may be baptized*—suffering, water, fire, the Body of Christ, and the Holy Spirit. now this,...

Paul's letters tend to emphasize Spirit-baptism over water-baptism. Paul said Abraham's *flesh-circumcision* foreshadowed *New-Testament-circumcision of the spirit. And the faith which rendered Abraham righteous before God was in his spirit BEFORE he got circumcised in his flesh!* Colossians 2:11 calls circumcision-of-the-spirit a baptism: *We who are in Christ are circumcised with the CIRCUMCISION-MADE-WITHOUT-HANDS; in putting off the-body-of-the-sins-of-the-flesh, by the circumcision of Christ. Flesh-circumcision is MADE WITH HANDS, while spirit-circumcision is made WITHOUT HANDS.* Baptism in water is always accomplished by a minister's hands; so water-baptism must not be what places one into the Body of Christ! *Salvation is a Holy-Spirit-operation!*

Romans 2:28-29: The circumcision which produces salvation occurs in a person's spirit, not in one's flesh. Philippians 3:3 says *believers are the circumcision who worship God in the spirit, and have no confidence in the flesh. Water-baptism affecting flesh only, and not spirit, put no UNDUE-CONFIDENCE in water-baptism!* And,...

Peter penned: "*BAPTISM NOW saves us (not putting away the filth of our flesh* [by water], *but the answer of a GOOD-CONSCIENCE toward God) by the resurrection of Jesus Christ.*" (1 Peter 3:21) Conscience, not flesh, is what this verse is about. *Water-baptism does not touch the conscience!* Hebrews 9:14 *assures us it is the shed-blood of Christ that purges our CONSCIENCE from sins!* Water cannot reach one's inner-man. Paul commanded in Colossians 2:6: "*JUST AS you have RECEIVED Jesus into your life, IN THAT SAME WAY WALK IN HIM.*" So, *if water-baptism is HOW we receive Christ, to CONTINUE IN HIM, we must be water-baptized every day! WE RECEIVE JESUS BY FAITH; AND CONTINUE IN HIM THE SAME WAY—BY FAITH!* (2 Corinthians 5:7) Abraham was and is our chief-faith-example!

Romans 4:9-12 says *Abraham's FAITH was counted as righteousness BEFORE God; BEFORE Abraham was circumcised!* Circumcision did not make Abraham right with God. *It was his FAITH that secured right-standing in the Creator's eyes. Circumcision SEALED THE DEAL!* "Abraham received the *SIGN* of circumcision; a *SEAL* of the righteousness of the *FAITH* which he had while he was *uncircumcised.*" *The logical-scriptural-conclusion of such good-news is*—Even as God declared Abraham in right-standing with Him before his circumcision—New-Covenant-Christians are saved prior to water-baptism! *Abraham's circumcision in his flesh foreshadowed our New-Covenant-baptism into Christ by the Holy Spirit.* (1 Corinthians 12:13, Colossians 2:11-12) *Water-baptism OUTWARDLY-pictures that previous-INNER-occurrence.*

In the Old Covenant, *sacrificial-blood was sprinkled on ITEMS to be ritually-purified.* Under Mosaic-law, *the blood of goats and cattle was sprinkled on physical and material-objects.* Hebrews 10:22: *We believers have our HEART sprinkled with the blood of Jesus from an EVIL-CONSCIENCE; and our bodies washed with pure-water. PURE-WATER being difficult to find on this planet, that statement must refer to "The washing of WATER by the WORD OF GOD."* (Ephesians 5:26) A different-kind-of-blood; and a different-kind-of-water! Christians are not to be immersed in Christ's blood; *BUT* sprinkled with it—nor to be sprinkled with water—*BUT* immersed in it. *Our SPIRIT is sprinkled with the blood of Jesus Christ; and our immersion in water is our acknowledgement of our death, burial and resurrection with Jesus Christ!*

What if a person accepts Jesus as Savior but cannot get to water because he or she lives in the frozen-north? Should he or she DIE BEFORE spring-thaw, is he or she forever lost? What about the crucified-thief, who asked the Lord to remember him when entering His Kingdom? He having not been *water-baptized* in Jesus' name, did he go to Hell when he died that day? Unlike the *water-baptism-heretics*, Jesus told him he would be with Him in Paradise that day! *What about all the Old-Covenant-Saints who had not been baptized in water or in Jesus' name?* Were they *DENIED* heaven? Check out Matthew 27:52-53, Ephesians 4:8 and Hebrews 12:22-24.

My purpose is neither to undermine water-baptism, nor to assign it a significance the Bible does not give it. *Over the years I have crossed paths with more than one church-member who had been taught to trust in water-baptism for salvation, instead of a personal-relationship with Jesus Christ; and I know that ONE was gloriously-saved when presented with Bible-Truth about the issue.* Moreover, I continue to get responses to my You-Tube-Bible-teaching-videos from some people who have been greatly-damaged by that water-baptism-heresy.

I have books on other *erroneous-teachings* plaguing the church today. Find them on ronaldcraigbooks.com. *ALL heresies have this common-flaw—Falsehoods cater to fleshly-desires, while claiming a Godly-lifestyle. And many churches tolerate such, to make it easy to get and keep church-members. Setting their standards too high might limit their member-number, income, and prestige. Pleasing people is more important than pleasing God for those who fear men instead of God; and look to men for their rewards.* (John 5:44, 12:42-43) In conclusion,...

Water-baptism, being a command of Christ, it is to our advantage to obey His command. But, Scripture is clear that outward-activity does not produce salvation. It is *believing* what Christ did on that cross. *Christians submit to water-baptism after having been regenerated. Faith connects one to God—not being bodily-submerged under the chemical consisting of one part Hydrogen two parts Oxygen.* Connect that with Jeremiah 2:22!

Now let us look at *BIBLE-TRUTH* about redemption. After all, *God wrote the book on it!* The Gospel is simple to *ALL* who meet its simple-demands. *Failure to receive salvation is DUE NOT TO any flaw in God's-plan; but to either IGNORANCE or UNBELIEF on the part of man.*

Chapter Seventeen

Legal and vital-sides of redemption

It is regrettable that it has been necessary to spend a whole chapter to expose the falsehood that one must be immersed in water before that one is actually saved. When Nehemiah faced the enormous-task of rebuilding those ruined-walls of Jerusalem, *he first had to remove mounds of rubbish from the original-building-site. Only AFTER hauling away all of the troublesome-trash could the returning-Jews begin to erect those walls on SOLID-GROUND.* (Nehemiah 2:13-18, 4:2, 10) Chapter-sixteen has *EXPOSED* and *REMOVED* a similar pile of rubbish. So now we can build our faith on solid-biblical-ground. *Trash-removal being exhausting, and distasteful, many church-leaders bypass that workload, and ATTEMPT to build God's house on the flimsy-foundation of hand-me-down-religious-doctrines.* They need to learn the lesson many building-contractors have learned the hard way: *Erecting an edifice on faulty-groundwork will eventually come back to haunt the builder!* See 2 Timothy 2:15 to get the biblical-significance of that harsh-reality.

I have learned to depend on God's-Written-Word for the answer to every-human-need. But, *even though the Bible offers genuine-relief to sufferers around the world, there is more suffering on earth today than ever before.* Despite the fact that more copies of Holy Scripture are available to people today, than that of any other book, and available in more languages, than any other book, many church-members are just as bereft of the truths of the Gospel as are unbelievers! *For that reason alone, I present this volume to the Body of Christ at large!*

Believers should know better than anyone else that the blessings Jesus purchased with His shed-blood do not automatically manifest; even in the life of believers. Deuteronomy 28:1-2 *linked all the blessings under the Old Covenant to the obedience of the participants of the Covenant: Those blessings would come on and overtake all who OBEYED the commands of the Covenant.* To the contrary, Deuteronomy 28:15-68 *promised only curses to ALL under the covenant who disobeyed the covenant-requirements: "All of these curses will come on you, and will overtake you."* But, *generally, neither the blessings nor the curses manifest in people's lives at the time they obey or disobey God's commands. But they will!!!*

The New Covenant is FAR-BETTER than the Old one was—with a BETTER-Mediator, BETTER-promises, and a BETTER-sacrifice. (Hebrews 7:22, 8:6-7, 9:23, 11:40) *Yet New-Covenant-rules are about the same: Obedience INVITES the blessings—disobedience WHISTLES for the curses—just as in days-of-old.* However, *rules for New-Covenant-Believers are a bit-stricter than those of Old-Covenant-Saints.* (Hebrews 2:1-3) *The volume of Bible-Truth available today renders excuses inexcusable.*

The salvation provided for us in Christ's sacrifice is just like the Sword of the Spirit—being double-edged—*having both LEGAL and VITAL-SIDES. The legal-side of redemption is the part having already taken place in the spirit-realm! Jesus purchased our redemption in-full for spirit, soul, body,* etc. Every-blessing was paid for long ago by our Lord's death on the cross—then secured by His resurrection from the dead. (Romans 5:10) Further sacrifice is unnecessary! God looks upon our salvation as a finished-product. Remember, *God calls things that are not yet as though they already were.* (Romans 4:17) In the beginning, God released out of His mouth things that did not exist in this universe; but which afterward appeared on earth and in space. (Genesis 1:3, 6, 9, 11, 14, 20, 24, 26) So, our believing things with our heart, then releasing what we believe with verbal-consistency is heaven's modus-operandi. Applying that principle to the New Covenant, God Himself believed and confessed that our Lord's sacrifice was more than enough for our complete-redemption! (John 3:16, etc., etc., etc.)

After Adam's sin and fall, our Creator searched this planet over for someone He could trust. After centuries of searching God finally found Abram (*meaning exalted father*); renaming him Abraham (*father of a multitude*). (Genesis 17:1-5, 2 Chronicles 16:9, Romans 4:17-18) *Abraham's constant-confession of that Divine-revelation assured that each time he mentioned his new-name, he was calling things that did not exist as though they did; LIKE his Creator did in the beginning. Abraham's words eventually MATERIALIZED; just like the Creator's words had done; AND AS HE PROMISED ABRAHAM'S WORDS WOULD. ABRAHAM LITERALLY BECAME THE FATHER OF MANY NATIONS BY BELIEVING AND SPEAKING the words God had spoken over him—then commanded him to believe and speak*: The Romans 10:9-10-principle.

Abraham DID NOT FIRST IMAGINE what he desired of God, and then CUNNINGLY-CONVINCE his Creator to grant his personal-wishes. God promised the blessings first—and that GAVE SUBSTANCE to those words in the mouth of Abraham—who cooperated with God's plan by consistently calling himself Abraham rather than Abram—his original name—a vital-Bible-Principle: One cannot say anything one pleases and expect blessings to bless. We are to believe and confess ONLY the words God has established in heaven (Psalms 119:89, Matthew 18:18); *which manifests the blessings on earth!*

Moreover, *we must believe and confess God's words not sporadically, nor experimentally, BUT AS A BRAND-NEW-WAY-OF-LIFE! THE VITAL-SIDE OF REDEMPTION IS OUR EXPERIENCING THE REDEMPTIVE-BLESSINGS JESUS CHRIST BOUGHT FOR US ON THE CROSS; AND OBVIOUSLY WANTS ALL BELIEVERS TO EXPERIENCE!* According to 2 Peter 3:9, *God does not want anyone to perish—but wants everyone to repent and be saved.* In fact, *God wants everyone to be saved AND come to the FULL-KNOWLEDGE of biblical-truth about the blessings Jesus purchased for us by His sacrifice.* (1 Timothy 2:4) Jesus was The Lamb of God Who took away the sins of the whole-world: (John 1:29) *And then commanded His disciples to preach that GOOD-NEWS to EVERYBODY in the whole-world.* (Mark 16:15) Nevertheless,...

Although God desires everybody on earth to be born again (and made the new-birth possible for everybody), *many leave this earth-realm UNPREPARED for the next.* Moreover, *Christ provided HEALING for our body in His Calvary-sacrifice* (Isaiah 53:4-5, 10, Matthew 8:16-17, Galatians 3:13); *yet most believers suffer from devilish-diseases.* In addition, *although Jesus made provision in that sacrifice for our material and financial-needs to be FULLY-SUPPLIED* (2 Corinthians 8:9, Philippians 4:19), *most modern-church-members look to the world to meet their needs, instead of to CHRIST'S-CROSS-PROVISION.* But now, let us go back in time for more revelation,...

Christ's cross-sacrifice—*which paid the full-price for our full-redemption* (for this life and the next), had been *PLANNED* from time-immemorial. Acts 2:23 tells us He was: "*Delivered* [up to be crucified] *by the determinate-counsel and foreknowledge of God.*" God ALWAYS knew what He was GOING to do! Revelation 13:8 *calls Christ the Lamb of God, Who was slain from the FOUNDATION of the world—FOUNDATION referring not to the creation of this-present-world, but to the destruction of Lucifer's kingdom—which event occurred on the earth long before Adam and Eve were created.* Lots of Scriptures clearly corroborate that pre-history. Such as the following,...

The Greek word *kataboolee*, rendered FOUNDATION in English in Matthew 13:35, 25:34, Luke 11:50, John 17:24, Ephesians 1:4, Hebrews 4:3, 9:26, 1 Peter 1:20, Revelation 13:8, 17:8; refers to that violent-destruction of "The world that then was." (2 Peter 3:6) *That cannot refer to Noah's-flood, because verses-five and seven tell us earth AND heaven were involved in that catastrophe*; whereas, in Noah's-flood only the earth was negatively-affected. Psalms 104:5-7 refers to the original-creation; *then to the flooding of the earth after Lucifer's rebellion*: "God laid the foundations of the earth so that it should not be moved forever. [But *THEN*] *You covered the earth with the DEEP* [Genesis 1:2] *like a garment*: The waters stood above the mountains. *At Your rebuke, they FLED: At the voice of Your thunder, THE WATERS HASTENED AWAY." In Noah's-flood the water did not hasten away! It took months.* (Genesis 8:3) Genesis 1:2, Isaiah 45:18 and Jeremiah 4:23 *all describe this planet as it existed before Adam and Eve existed.* Scripture establishes the fact that some pre-Adamite social-system existed upon this planet in the far-distant-past! If not, the Scripture passages we looked at make no sense at all.

The Greek kataboolee occurs in Hebrews 11:11 too, *but was rendered CONCEIVE there; referring to Sarah's pregnancy with Isaac.* Conception could not have been what the writer of Hebrews intended. *Conception* would be *taking in* seed, whereas kataboolee means *TO CAST DOWN*. Therefore, *birthing seed into the world would be a better translation. Sarah CAST FORTH seed out of her womb.* Therefore, *that Greek word kataboolee obviously signifies the very same in each of those references—the THROWING DOWN OF—NOT THE CREATION OF.*

If the word KATABOOLEE refers to original-creation, and means that—AT creation God foreordained Christ's death, that would suggest that both sin and redemption were in God's original-plans for creation—John Calvin's demonic-theology! The cross-death BECAME necessary AFTER sin invaded the universe—AFTER CREATION!

The general-Greek-word for foundation is *themelios.* Hebrews 9:26 says that *if Christ's sacrifice had been as powerless to remove sins as was the blood of bulls and goats, He would have had to suffer often from* (or after) *the kataboolee* (overthrow) *of that world* (-system under the fallen-Lucifer)—*not from the themelios* (founding) *of the earth.* Neither Adam's nor Satan's fall was included in God's original-plans for creation! That means,...

If God never meant for sin to exist, then redemption would not have been necessary either! Our Creator did not plan man's fall and redemption the day He created heaven and earth. In fact, *God never planned any kind of failure for any creature!* But, Lucifer rebelled against God and His rules—*intending to build his own kingdom from those materials the Creator had brought into being! The devil used the same deceptive-tools against man on earth as he did against a third of the angels in heaven.* Therefore, of necessity, God initiated plans to *REDEEM* everything that was *REDEEMABLE.* Of course, Lucifer, now the devil, other fallen angels and demons were not redeemable-creatures. Matthew 8:29, 25:41, 1 Timothy 5:21, 2 Peter 2:4, Jude 6 and Revelation 20:10 *PROVE* that truth! *Those angelic-beings rebelled in the blazing-light-of-truth. They INVENTED SIN*; because sin existed *NOWHERE* in God's universe before then.

Matthew 25:41 *does not say that God CREATED the Lake of Fire for LUCIFER and other UNLUCKY-ANGELS; but that God PREPARED the Lake of Fire for THE DEVIL AND OTHER ANGELS THAT REBELLED WITH HIM.* So, *the Lake of Fire did not come into existence at creation. It was PREPARED AFTER CREATION for punishment of those angelic-rebels.* But, Jesus said in Matthew 25:41 that *unrepentant-human-rebels will rate a similar-fate.*

Hebrews 6:1 *put kataboolee and themelios together, warning believers to NOT CAST DOWN (kataboolee) the original-FOUNDATION (themelios) of the Christian-faith. The writer was urging us to go on to perfection from the foundation (themelios) of the faith, instead of destroying faith and trying to start over again. Hebrews 6:4-6 says it is impossible to rebuild the Christian-faith in one's life after DELIBERATELY tearing down that faith!*

The Creator KNEW from the beginning of angelic and human-history how their history will end. (Isaiah 46:10) Yet, *GOD KNOWING THE END OF HISTORY FROM THE BEGINNING OF IT DOES NOT PROVE OR EVEN IMPLY THAT GOD PLANNED EVERYTHING THAT HAPPENS IN HISTORY!* Ephesians 3:10-11: "*To the intent that NOW, unto the principalities and powers [BOTH good and bad angels] in the heavenlies might be known by the church the manifold-wisdom of God—and that according to the eternal-purpose that God purposed in Christ Jesus our Lord.*" *Why does God need to PROVE His wisdom to the angels—UNLESS some angels challenged His authority?* An event our Creator never planned. But, neither did it take Him off guard. (Proverbs 15:3) Therefore,...

It is MORE-BIBLICAL to believe God used the church to demonstrate His great-wisdom to those angels (both good and evil) *AFTER sin invaded the universe than it is to believe He planned for some creatures to be sinners!*

Since God placed both the tree of life and the tree of knowledge of good and evil in the Garden of Eden, it is evident that sin had already made its debut somewhere in the universe before Adam and Eve were created. So, Adam and Eve were faced with two-*OPPOSING*-options. Since evil was already *IN* the universe, *mankind had to be tested to demonstrate either loyalty to the Creator, or loyalty to an enemy. God having given Adam the ability and responsibility to choose, He assumed responsibility for Adam when Adam chose wrong.* And, that is one of the purposes of redemption! But, Lucifer was given no option, other than to obey his Creator's commands; for evil did not already exist in God's universe. Lucifer was not a robot, however; he had ability to make decisions; and he deliberately-decided to rebel against God.

Angels obviously can make choices—for Lucifer and other angels made some *UNWISE*-choices. (2 Peter 2:4, Jude 6) *Lucifer's rebellion was initiated within himself.* He envisioned a career that could not exist—and using the resources God Himself had invested in Lucifer—his *BEAUTY AND WISDOM*—to challenge his own Creator's *RIGHT* to maintain dominion in His very own universe. (Isaiah 14:12-15, Ezekiel 28:12-18) Such treason was unforgivable. Now the bottom line,...

The *LEGAL-side* of redemption is *God's-part* of that plan. Some theologians have twisted certain Scriptures into a theological-system of *predetermination*; claiming that God *ARBITRARILY-PREDESTINED SOME* people to be *SAVED*, and others *LOST*—*the individuals having no choice in the matter.* One example is Ephesians 1:4, 11; *which does say some were PREDESTINED to salvation.* One more is 2 Thessalonians 2:13: *"God has from the beginning CHOSEN YOU to salvation."* Romans 9:21 is another passage they distort: *"Has not the Potter* [God] *power over the clay* [people] *FROM THE SAME LUMP TO*

MAKE ONE VESSEL TO BE HONORABLE AND ANOTHER TO BE DISHONORABLE?"* Second Timothy 2:20-21 settles it: *"In a great house, SOME vessels are made to honor, OTHERS to dishonor. If one PURGES HIMSELF from the [dishonorable-things], then that one will be a vessel to HONOR, and sanctified and fit for the master's use; one prepared for every good work."* On the basis of Romans 9:21 alone, we could get the wrong idea that God really is arbitrary in selecting redemption-recipients. But, by comparing Romans 9:21 to 2 Timothy 2:20-21 we get a different view on the subject. *People have a part in their redemption—receiving it by THEIR faith and obedience. Predestination refers to what people will become if they get born again—not to some arbitrary-choice of who will be SAVED and who UNSAVED. Predestination is not the CAUSE of one's salvation; but the RESULT of exercising faith for salvation!* Because Scripture says plainly,...

"God is not willing that ANYONE perish, but that ALL will repent, and be saved." (2 Peter 3:9) "God will have *EVERYONE* to be saved." (1 Timothy 2:4) Hebrews 2:9: "By God's grace, Christ tasted death for *EVERYBODY."* Hebrews 9:12: "By His own blood, Christ entered once into the Holy-Place in heaven; *having obtained eternal-redemption for EVERYONE who will believe."* Thus,...

God withholds no blessing from anybody who meets His conditions. (Psalms 84:11, Romans 8:32) Yet, many fail to receive the benefits of God's redemption-plan! In Luke 13:23 someone asked Christ: "Lord, are there few that will be saved?" The Lord's answer: "Strive to enter at the narrow-gate: For many will seek to enter in, and will not be able." *What is the entrance-gate?* Jesus said in John 10:9: *"I AM THE DOOR:* By Me, if one enters in *HE WILL BE SAVED."* Confirmed in Acts 4:12: "There is salvation in *NO OTHER* than Jesus Christ: For there is no other name under heaven, *having been given among* men [on earth], *whereby we are to be saved.*" "Whoever believes that Jesus is the Christ has been born of God [has entered God's Kingdom]." (1 John 5:1) "Christ has become the author of eternal-salvation to *EVERYBODY* who obeys Him." (Hebrews 5:9) As for non-obeyers,...

Hebrews 2:3: "How can *WE* escape [punishment for our sins], if *WE* neglect so-great-salvation?" We have to *LAY HOLD OF* salvation by faith and confession—meet the conditions. Salvation is not arbitrarily-distributed!

"God is the Savior of all men; *specially of those who believe.*" (1 Timothy 4:10) *Although salvation has been made available to all, only those who believe the Gospel receive those Gospel-benefits. The Greek word rendered specially means in-particular, or to-the-greatest-degree. The ones who in-particular believe the Gospel-message will receive salvation to-the-greatest-degree!* Of course, *the opposite is true of Gospel-spurners.* Christ-rejecters will be heirs of Hebrews 10:26-31—unless they repent!

The LEGAL-SIDE of redemption is Christ's-sacrifice. And His sacrificial-blood is safe in heaven's-depository. (Hebrews 9:12) *To receive from that deposit, we have to confess with our mouth Jesus is Lord and believe in our heart that God has raised Him from the dead.* (Romans 10:9-10) *The VITAL-SIDE of redemption is our receiving what was achieved by the LEGAL-SIDE on the cross!*

Why would heaven invest so much time and effort to achieve only partial-redemption—and that for a limited-number of people? Ephesians 3:20 says God is able to, and Hebrews 7:25 says He does, save to the uttermost!

The next and final chapter goes deeper into the vital-side of redemption—based on the seed-principle, which God built into creation right at the beginning.

Chapter Eighteen

God's eternal-seed-principle

In light of the Bible-Truth that a complete-salvation has been provided for the *ENTIRE*-population of earth, *it has to be possible for each and every human being on the planet to be born again, and to experience complete-victory in every-phase of life* (in this evil-age); *and then inhabit heaven.* Mankind in general, however, does not bask in those blessings: Even most believers! Why not? *Although there are more reasons for FAILURE to receive redemptive-blessings than any unbeliever or believer is willing to admit, no such reason implicates The Provider of redemptive-blessings!* Because: *"GOD IS FOR US and not against us."* (Romans 8:31) Why would God provide the redemptive-blessings, and then hide them from us, or try to keep us from receiving them? Not only that,...

Satan, who wants to deprive everyone of every New-Covenant-blessing (1 Peter 5:8) *has NO AUTHORITY to* defraud believers of Divine-goodness! Both John 12:31 and 16:11 tell us that *Satan is now an OUTCAST. That assures us he has NO ABILITY to cheat anybody out of any Gospel-benefit who meets the Gospel-requirements.*

Yet, *the devil has managed to deprive even believers of MANY redemptive-blessings BY stealthily-planting in the church MANY-religious-traditions that cheat untold-numbers of believers of countless-redemptive-blessings; convincing them Scripture really means something other than what it truly says; or, for some mysterious-reason, God rescinded some of those redemptive-blessings prior to modern-times. Many Christians FORFEIT their blood-*

bought-blessings, either through religious-deceptions, or by their own outright-refusal to believe the Gospel. Even Eve said *the subtle-Serpent BEGUILED her* (Genesis 3:13); and believers today should not naively-think our enemy has abandoned that deceptive-tool that worked so well on Eve. Satan either *persuades people to reject the Gospel outright; OR turns the Gospel into something it is not through religious-lies.* The enemy first attempts to keep people away from the Gospel—if at all possible. *He knows if they are not exposed to Gospel-Truth, they will more likely not take hold of its benefits.* That ploy is three-pronged: *The devil either tempts God's messenger to quit preaching the Gospel, or compromise the Gospel.* Or, *he allures the once-obedient-messenger into sin and disrepute, in order to both discredit AND disqualify that ministry.* Or, *he offers excuses to the potential-hearers, so they WILL SHIELD THEMSELVES from Gospel-Truth.* (Luke 14:16-24) Gospel-Truth reaches some no matter what the devil does; so if his first attempts fail, he then activates plan *B—sneaking in unnoticed to pervert the Gospel the new-believer just received.* (Galatians 1:6-8, 2:4, Jude 3-4) But, Scripture demands that we give the devil *NO PLACE!* (Ephesians 4:27) And now this,...

The biblical-seed-principle is also known as the law-of-sowing-and-reaping. The seed-principle affects every creature on earth—biological and botanical. In Genesis chapter-one, God *CREATED* plants, insects, fish, birds, animals and human beings; *and instructed them all to REPRODUCE after their own kind. Therefore, it was the Creator Who instituted that all-pervasive-seed-principle; which is absolutely-essential for all living-things.* So,...

The next time you are out driving, you need to drive safely; *but also notice how many objects you behold are dependent on that seed-principle for survival—let alone perpetuation.* What if our Creator, Who originated that seed-principle in the beginning, *repealed His universal-seed-principle?* Man's fragile-world would suddenly fall apart. Every life-form would eventually disappear. *That assures us that life itself is a manifestation of the seed-principle: Living-beings cannot LIVE without it!*

If grass no longer yielded seed, pasturelands would soon perish; *making the earth barren-terrain.* Foraging-fauna would hasten the process by consuming most of the disappearing-greenery, while trampling all the rest. Inability of animals to reproduce, combined with man's *carnivorous-consumption* would soon deplete the meat-supply, and further accelerate the extermination of the animal-kingdom. The scarcity of vegetables and grains would increase the demand on supply of stored-goods. Thus, mankind would soon be facing starvation!

Dying-house-pets would eliminate man's enjoyment of tail-wagging and purring around the house; with no prospect of replacing those treasured-friends. Because humankind would be under the same curse, fewer and fewer households would be graced with children. Many would likely not live long anyway; food-supplies shortly being depleted. Tragically, as in bygone-times, and still prevalent in some locales on earth today, cannibalism would become an unpleasant-reality. *Survival depends upon that Divine-principle of sowing seeds and reaping harvests!* (The same is true of that Divine-redemption-package; as we will soon see.) But continuing this,...

Skyrocketing-prices of those limited-supplies would accelerate the threat of total-lifelessness on the planet. Disappearing-forests would bring *home-construction* to a standstill. And, *factory-output* would be hampered by the lack of natural and human-resources. There would likely still be plenty of vehicles around; but there being shortages of petroleum-products due to reduced-ability to manufacture them, how many of them would still beusable? Reduced-demand for transport-services would eliminate more jobs. And, why keep shops open to sell merchandise to those who are bereft of even the basic-necessities-of-life—they having no money to shop—and no means of generating income to shop! And yet,...

As *unthinkable* as those afore-mentioned-conditions might be, *those unpleasantries refer ONLY to the lethal-effects of the sudden-suspension of God's reproductive-laws in the natural-realm. But, what about one's inner-essence? The unsaved may be saved only by spiritual-rebirth—that too requiring some reproductive-dynamics. Thus, the seed-principle is absolutely-essential, even in the spirit-realm. Salvation springs from planting Gospel-SEEDS in human-hearts.* (Mark 4:13-20, 1 Peter 1:23)

Thus, words themselves are seeds—albeit spiritual-ones. Even Christ Himself—the Word of God (John 1:1, Revelation 19:13)—is a *SEED*. (Genesis 3:15, Galatians 3:16) *The very Kingdom of God operates by the sowing-and-reaping-law!* Check out Mark 4:26-31. Were it not for the seed-principle, there would even be no need for Scripture, preaching, or church-meetings. Humankind would have no future-hope—and little reason to live on earth now. Thus, our existence in both body and spirit is tied to God's eternal-seed-principle! But hold on,...

Believe it or not, the seed-principle extends further: For even the resurrection of our bodies depends on the sowing-and-reaping-law. Paul said: *"The body is SOWN* [So even our bodies are *SEEDS.*] *in corruption; and it is raised in incorruption."* (1 Corinthians 15:42) Moreover, *even our own personal-Christian-maturity is dependent on that seed-principle*: "You are God's husbandry [field, farm, garden]." (1 Corinthians 3:9) *So, God continues to SOW SEEDS OF GOSPEL-TRUTH INTO US EVEN AFTER WE GET BORN AGAIN! Living-Word-SEEDS even HELP us keep our lives PURE: "Whoever is born of God does not commit sin—because, His SEED* [Word] *remains in him: And he cannot sin because he has been born of God."* (1 John 3:9) No escaping our need for seed! Also,...

In 2 Corinthians, chapters-eight and nine, we learn that *MONEY GIVEN by the believers in one city to some believers in Judea, who had some dire-economic-needs was counted as SEED. Money-gifts were planted-seeds that would grant a harvest of like-kind for the planters!*

Genesis 8:22 permanently-established that sowing-and-reaping-law: *"While the earth remains, SEEDTIME-AND-HARVEST WILL NOT CEASE."* So whether we seek natural or spiritual-solutions for any of our situations, that sowing-and-reaping-*LAW* is an absolute-necessity! We also must be careful what we sow, because we reap harvests from whatever *KIND* of seeds we sow—good or bad. (Galatians 6:7-10) On top of all that,...

I have found that redemption is both *instantaneous* and *progressive.* Our new-birth is only the beginning of our salvation-experience; because our salvation is both *initiated* and *consummated* by that seed-principle. The Lord said God's Kingdom is entered by one having His Living-Word *PLANTED* in one's spirit. (Matthew 13:3-9, 18-23) His words are *LIVING-SEEDS* (Luke 8:11, John 1:1-4, 6:63, Hebrews 4:12) producing their *OWN KIND.* Matthew chapter-thirteen teaches that God's words are *spiritual-seeds sown in people's spirits—proper-soil for spiritual-seeds.* Christ then taught on Satan's attempts *to thwart the purpose for which such seeds are sown*: A rich-harvest for both God and believers. If God loses a good-crop He was expecting, then believers also forfeit a bountiful-harvest. *The purpose of seeds is HARVEST!*

Matthew chapter-thirteen catalogs *THE STUNTS* the devil pulls on Gospel-hearers. When that Word is sown on *calloused-hearts* (hard-packed-soil), the devil comes immediately and removes the Gospel-seeds before they interact with *SPIRIT-SOIL*. (Matthew 13:19, Mark 4:15) Seeds sown on *rocky-ground* (such as the cotton-fields I used to work in long ago) might *SPROUT* immediately, especially if it has recently rained. Thin-moist-soil atop a rock in the sunlight is prime-condition for sprouting; but not for rooting—necessary for both endurance and fruit-production. (Matthew 13:20-22) Another soil-type is thorn-infested-ground. Such soil contains seeds that are hostile to Gospel-Seeds. The lust for things, worry, and deceptions about money deprive the Gospel-Seeds of the necessary nutrition to survive; let alone produce fruit. (Joshua 1:8, Proverbs 4:20-27, Luke 8:15, John 15:1-8) Some hearts are productive-soil. "Good-ground is that one who hears the Gospel, understands it, and *BEARS FRUIT—some a hundredfold; some sixty; some thirty.*" (Matthew 13:23) *So, even good-ground varies in productivity-levels. But good-ground is THE ONLY SOIL that produces fruit!* To make sure you are a productive-field, read and heed Jeremiah 4:3. Furthermore,...

In order to be saved, people must first acknowledge that they *NEED* to be saved. *And such acknowledgment is the result of Holy-Spirit-CONVICTION.* (John 16:8-11) "*Godly-sorrow produces repentance to salvation; not to be repented of* [Repenters do not regret repenting!]: *But the sorrow of the world produces death.*" (2 Corinthians 7:10) In worldly-sorrow, the violator is sorry for getting caught. It is not real-repentance! As for the timing,...

"*NOW IS THE ACCEPTED-TIME* [for accepting Christ as one's Savior]—*NOW IS THE DAY OF SALVATION.*" (2 Corinthians 6:2) That means salvation is both an issue we cannot afford to ignore, or dismiss; and that *WHEN WE BELIEVE THE GOSPEL WE START RECEIVING THE BENEFITS IN THIS-LIFE.* Thus, *we do not have to WAIT until we get to heaven for some salvation-goodies.* John 5:24: "He who believes *HAS* eternal life." *Redemption is effective IN us the moment we believe in our heart that God raised Christ from the dead, then confess with our mouth that Jesus is Lord.* So says Romans 10:9-10.

Our Lord cautioned in Matthew 7:22-23: "Many will say unto Me on that day of judgment: 'Lord, Lord, have we not prophesied in Your name? And, in Your name cast out demons? And, in Your name have done many wonderful works [in their estimation, of course]?' Then will I declare to them: *'I never KNEW you*: Depart from Me, you who work iniquity.'" It is tragic that many who *BELIEVE* they will inhabit heaven upon their death will be unpleasantly-surprised, *after it is too late to remedy their eternal-predicament.* So many have chosen a path leading to destruction, by listening to false-prophets; *WOLVES* disguising themselves as *SHEEP* (Matthew 7:15)—who have convinced them to believe that they are on the True-Gospel-Path, when in reality they are on a downward path toward Hell. Did the rich-Jewish-man who mistreated Lazarus think that he would be a future-resident of that fiery region? *The devil yet seeks for and finds fools!* (Proverbs 14:12, 16:25)

The only way to be sure we are putting our trust in Gospel-Truth *and not in religious-tradition is to*: "*Study to show ourselves approved unto God* [and not man]; *a workman who needs not to be ashamed; BECAUSE we rightly-divide the Word of Bible-Truth.*" (2 Timothy 2:15) *If honest-Bible-research assures the right-rendering of God's Word, dishonest Bible-study will end in wrongly-rendering Bible-Truth!* THEREFORE, DARE TO COMPARE WHAT

YOU BELIEVE ALREADY WITH THE HOLY SCRIPTURES! Paul told us to: "*Examine yourselves whether you are in the faith; prove your own selves.*" (2 Corinthians 13:5) Make *SURE* you are sowing proper-seeds into your heart. Securing your eternal-welfare is worth putting forth that much effort! Acts 17:11-12 describes wise-hearers. Check that out.

What is the Divine-purpose of Christians abiding in Christ? "*Those whom God foreknew* [by Divine-insight], *He predestinated TO BE CONFORMED TO THE IMAGE OF HIS SON, so that He might be firstborn among many brethren.*" *Christ expects CHRISTians to represent Him in every aspect of life—and not just engage in religious-routine. The Lord rightly-expects saint-fruit from saints!* (John 15:1-8, Galatians 5:16-26) As for hypocrites,...

Mark 7:7: "*In VAIN they worship Me* [God]; *teaching as doctrine human-commands* [replacing God's Word]." And heaven's response—Matthew 21:43: "*The Kingdom of God will be taken away from you* [Israel], *and given to a nation* [the church—1 Peter 2:9] *that produces the fruit* [God expects]." And not only the Jewish-leaders, but even "If the Christian-believer abides not in Me [Christ], he will be cast forth as a [once-living-but-now-dead] branch, and will wither; and the angels will gather them, and cast them into the fire of Hades; and they will burn [forever]." (John 15:6—Speaking of Christians who do not keep God's Word seeds inside them!) Also read Romans 11:11-22 and Hebrews 6:4-6. *If God spared not Israelites who rebelled—Christians beware!* For, God is no respecter of persons. Notice this too,...

Our new-birth does not put a stop to Satan's attacks on us. In fact, being in Christ provokes him to intensify his attacks; because we abandoned his lordship. Thus, we have to activate Ephesians 4:27 and James 4:7.

Philippians 2:12: "*WORK OUT* your own salvation." Paul did not say here that we are to *PRODUCE* our own salvation. Because Philippians 2:13 explains that: "*It is God Who works in you* [believers] *both to will and to do His good pleasure.*" Only God can work salvation in us: Only we can work our salvation out. *We believers have responsibility in both getting saved and staying saved. Our part is to WORK OUT the salvation which God has WORKED IN US, by believing, confessing, and obeying His Word. And the Holy Spirit even helps us do that!*

In Matthew 13:3-8 and 18-23, the sower sowed the same-kind-of-seed on four-different-kinds-of-soil. So it was not the seeds themselves that made the difference in productivity; *but the different-kinds-of-soil the seeds were sown in. The first-type of soil would not permit the seeds to penetrate its surface*—making it easy for birds to snatch them away. *The second-type of soil permitted the seeds only a limited-environment.* They were able to sprout, but had too little earth to provide moisture and other nutrients to remain alive; let alone produce fruit. *The third-type of soil received the seeds, then attacked them from within.* Thorn-plants resident in that ground absorbed all the nutrients and moisture—*depriving the good-seeds of everything they needed to produce. ONLY ONE of those FOUR-soil-types becomes productive; and that with time. Moreover, even that fourth-type varies in productivity-levels—one-hundred; sixty; thirtyfold!*

Our enemy uses certain tools to persuade Christians to loosen their grip on God's Word-seeds after they have been planted in their heart. Persecution and temptation pressure many to seek an *easier-lifestyle.* Yet, while no believer wants to turn against God's Word, *EXTREME-PRESSURE WORKS ON SOME BELIEVERS.* (John 6:66) *When a Christian starts looking for some lifestyle easier than Christianity sometimes turns out to be, Satan will accommodate them with certain-religious-traditions that seem to be genuine, but are instead satanic-substitutes: Combining a few biblical-terms with a generous-portion of catering-to-the-FLESH.* In 2 Corinthians 10:3-5, *Paul said believers must use spiritual-weapons to pull down EVERY satanic-stronghold.* Check out Ephesians 4:27, James 4:7 and 1 Peter 5:8-9 as well. Summing up,...

The *LEGAL*-side of redemption includes God's-plan to *PROVIDE* redemption for Adam's fallen-descendants; and Christ's-sacrifice to *PURCHASE* redemption for all who grab hold of that redemption by faith; then the sending forth of anointed-*MESSENGERS* with good-news about the redemption God planned and Christ provided; and *HOLY-SPIRIT-CONVICTION* in the hearts of the hearers about that redemption provided for all who *BELIEVE*.

And that is the *VITAL*-side of redemption—believing the good-news about redemption—then, working it out by our faith and confession—and never letting go of it. *Jesus Christ sticks with believers who stick with Him!* (Matthew 10:32-33)

Now finally, a concise-compilation of the components of current-crises complicating circumstances confronting the complete-citizenship of this world in the culmination of this compromising and confusing-age. WHEW!

Identity-crisis cause and cure in a nutshell

Both problems and solutions are laid out in consecutive-order here, but in a-concise-manner, as we summarize how life on this planet began, then went downhill, then was restored by Jesus Christ on Calvary's-cross:

Adam and Eve were at first *IDENTIFIED WITH GOD* (Luke 3:38); enjoying the privileges of their relationship with their Creator. Adam and Eve had it made—*having none of the problems of the modern-world.* They had no fear, worry, pain or scarcity in their paradise. Had they remained obedient to the Creator, then we today would have it made as well; because He both constructed and instructed Adam and Eve to *reproduce after their own kind.* (Genesis 1:26-28) All their descendants would be innocent and blessed to this day. But instead,...

Adam severed his relationship with his Creator and joined up with God's adversary—constituting the devil the-god-of-the-present-evil-age. (2 Corinthians 4:4) *By that SIN, Adam became IDENTIFIED WITH THE DEVIL.* (John 8:44) That unequal yoke has brought curse after curse upon this cursed-planet. (2 Corinthians 6:14-16) *God's punishment for their single-sin was to oust Adam and Eve from that paradise; THEN introduce them to an existence of fear, selfishness, and scarcity-of-blessings.* "Be sure *YOUR SIN* will find you out." (Numbers 32:23) *Not only were they ISOLATED from both God and Eden; they were forced to eke out a meager-existence from the very ground their sin had cursed!* They were not happy-campers. And, to make matters worse, *they now had to serve a cruel-god that not only failed to provide for them as their Creator had—but even sought their destruction. Adam UNIDENTIFIED HIMSELF FROM his Creator, then IDENTIFIED HIMSELF WITH a liar and murderer. Yet,...*

Humankind has attempted through its long-history to *DENY ANY CONNECTION* with Adam's fallen-nature. *While most refuse to acknowledge that inherited-nature, others, though admitting their sinful-constitution, invent systems of self-salvation*—philosophy, pagan-religions, science; even distorted-forms-of-Christianity. However, whatever face people put on themselves, that is merely a facade, by which they try to *HIDE* the *sinful-condition they inherited from fallen-Adam. The ONLY escape from the human-predicament is to admit one is a sinner, and accept God's ONE-means-of-redemption:* "Jesus Christ, and Him [having been] crucified." (1 Corinthians 2:2)

Adam's *perverted-condition* resulted from his union with Satan, the *chief-pervert*. Mankind was not morally flawed at creation! When the Creator said His creation was good He was speaking of Adam and Eve, as well as all other creatures. (Genesis 1:31) But that changed,...

For, since Adam had been constructed to reproduce after his own kind, *after he became the sinner-kind, he could ONLY produce the sinner-kind*. That problem has been passed down to every generation since. Thus,...

In every generation since Adam sinned: "The wrath of God is revealed from heaven against all ungodliness and unrighteousness of those who hold down the truth in unrighteousness. For, what may be known of God is manifest in them: For, God has showed it to them. For, all the invisible things of Him, from the creation of the world, are clearly seen—*being understood by the things that are made*; *His eternal-power and Godhead*; so that they are all without excuse: Because, when they knew God, they glorified Him not as God, nor were thankful, but became vain in their imagination; and their foolish heart was darkened. Professing themselves to be wise, they became fools instead. And, they changed the glory of the incorruptible-God into formed-images, like unto corruptible-humans, birds, fourfooted beasts and even creeping things. So, God gave them up to uncleanness through the lusts of their own hearts; to dishonor their own bodies among themselves. They also changed the truth of God into a lie, and worshipped and served the creation more than the One Who created creation. For that cause, God gave them up unto vile-affections; for, even their women did change the natural-use into that which is against nature: And likewise the men, leaving the natural-use of the woman, burned in their lust one toward another; men with men, working that which is improper; then receiving within themselves repayment for their error; that being proper on God's part. And as they had *NO DESIRE* to retain God in their knowledge, God gave them over to a reprobate-mind, to do what is improper in God's sight: *FILLED* with unrighteousness, fornication, wickedness, covetousness, maliciousness, envy, murder, deceit, malignity; and being whisperers, backbiters, haters of God, despiteful, proud, boasters, inventors of *EVIL* things; being disobedient to parents, without understanding, without *ANY* natural-affection, covenant-breakers, unmerciful: And although knowing the judgments of God, that all who do those things are worthy of death, not only do the same themselves, but have pleasure in other people who do them!" (Romans 1:18-32) That was how evil *BEGAN* on earth. But, Paul prophesied that evil men and imposters *WILL BECOME WORSE AND WORSE* (at the end of this-age); deceiving and being deceived. (2 Timothy 3:13) That prophecy is being fully-fulfilled today before our very eyes. And,...

The real issue in all of this is that the devil is out to *PERVERT AND TOTALLY-DESTROY EVERYTHING GOD CREATED. The former-Lucifer* (now Satan) *is attempting to get back at God for the eternal-judgment HE brought upon himself by his rebellion; which he and one third of the angels engaged in before Adam came along.* (That is another Bible-history-lesson, which is backed by many Scripture passages.) But back to our present,...

MODERN-WOKISM is an extreme-form of the devil's perversion-tactic. Wokism has perverted *EVERY* social-standard—primarily the biblical-family-structure. Male and female biblical-designations have been scrambled: *Many people know not WHAT they are—let alone WHO they are. Those Wokists have EVEN STOOPED to forcing children into attempted-sex-changes; even without their parents' consent; or even their knowledge of such event. On top of all that, drag-queen-perversion-shows are not only tolerated in public-school-systems, but demanded; and that even by federal, state, and local-governments!*

Considering *FALLEN-WORLD-HISTORY*, their falling into such demonic-traps is not surprising. *And, neither are their claims as to the reasons for modern-problems. Peter prophesied that, in the-last-days, SCOFFERS will arise; scoffing at everything decent and Godly.* (2 Peter 3:3) And, true to Peter's-prophecy: Wokists blame all of our problems *ON* climate-change, racism, Christianity, white-supremacy, capitalism, America, Israel, *AND* the Bible! But, the Bible trashes those Wokist-arguments: "*EARTH IS DEFILED under its inhabitants* [not because of the above, but,] *BECAUSE PEOPLE TRANSGRESSED GOD'S LAWS; HAVE CHANGED THE ORDINANCE OF GOD; AND BROKEN THE ETERNAL-COVENANT. It is for THOSE REASONS the curse has devoured the earth; so its inhabitants are desolate.*" (Isaiah 24:5-6) Plus,...

"The people will be oppressed, each one by another; each one by his neighbor: Children will behave proudly against the older [and wiser-]adults; and the worthless against the honorable." (Isaiah 3:5) But: "Woe to those who call evil good, and good evil; who put darkness for light, and light for darkness; who put bitter for sweet, and sweet for bitter! Woe to those who are wise in their *OWN* eyes and are prudent in their *OWN* sight!" (Isaiah 5:20-21) God's response: *"I will punish the world for its evil; and will punish the wicked for their iniquity. I will cause the arrogance of the proud to cease; and I will lay low the haughtiness of the terrible-ones."* (Isaiah 13:11) An account of this world's sin and punishment!

Yet, even more-surprising and thoroughly-disgusting is the fact that even some CHURCHES are hosting drag-queen-events for their congregation! How did the church come to SUCH A LOW STATE of understanding of, and commitment to, BOTH Almighty God AND Gospel-Truth? On my ronaldcraigbooks.com *website, more books with more Bible-Answers to that question are listed.* And this volume also provides a lot of biblical-information about the problems troubling this troubled-world; and about the Divine-solutions to those problems. To begin,...

God having appointed *MAN* as the *LEGAL*-guardian over the earth, then *ONLY A MAN* could *LEGALLY*-solve the problems of man. But, the problem-solver also had to have the *ABILITY* to handle the problem. Fallen-man had authority on earth; but being a fallen-creature, *HE HAD NO ABILITY TO MAKE MANKIND UN-FALLEN*. Our Creator had the *ABILITY* to solve that problem, but not the *AUTHORITY* to do so (as God), because He had put man in charge of earthly-affairs. *So, to legally-solve the problem, God had to visit our fallen-planet in man-form. GOD HAD TO BE BOTH ABLE AND LEGAL TO REDEEM*

MAN FROM HIS LOSTNESS AND THE DEVIL; WITHOUT DESTROYING THE MAN IN THE PROCESS. God became that man in the form of the Messiah. (Matthew 1:20-25, Luke 1:35, John 1:1, 14, Philippians 2:5-11) However, *to LEGALLY-solve the sin-problem, the Messiah had not only to come in human-flesh, but to become Adam in his sinful-state! He did such on the cross.* In 1 Corinthians 15:45-47 Paul called Christ the *Last-Adam. The Savior on the cross became everything Adam had become: SIN* (2 Corinthians 5:21), the *CURSE* (Galatians 3:13), *SICK* (Isaiah 53:4-5, 10, Matthew 8:16-17) and *POOR* (Isaiah 53:12, 2 Corinthians 8:9). *He having DIED in our place, the Lord's body was buried; but His Spirit descended to HADES, where He deposited our sins, curses, diseases, poverty and death.* When He rose from the dead, Jesus brought back with Him no sin or any of its vile-curses! *Thus, our being in Christ means we are separated from sin and those curses—experiencing the opposite of what Adam's sin brought upon the human race.* Christ had to actually *BECOME ADAM* on that cross, to get rid of the Adam in us! Yet, although salvation is available,...

More and more of our youth look to alcohol, drugs, so-called free-sex, video games, and many other thrills, in order to sooth their discomfort, loneliness, boredom, exclusion from some in-crowd; and to avoid being seen with family-members, or, having to admit their parents might be right after all. As for many parents, they want to escape their problem-kids, by burying themselves in *TV*-sit-coms, soap-operas, sports, pornography, buying stuff, yelling at one another, griping about government and taxes, etc. And whereas preachers are supposed to possess an educated-expertise on dealing with all such problems by personal-counseling, theological-sermons, etc; many of those preachers are *burning out* under the extreme-pressure, and leaving the ministry altogether.

ALL those conditions being politically-advantageous to unscrupulous-politicians—unscrupulous-politicians connive to get the votes to put and keep them in office; *where they run their own RAT-RACE.* On top of all that, the fake-news-media continually bombard the general-public with mountains of information that is often just as crooked as the claims of those people they blow the whistle on! Is there any way to get at actual-truth?

The *REAL*-problem on earth is *NOT* climate-change, or even Wokism; but that politics, business, education, news-gathering-and-dissemination, church-ministries, and even family-life *OPERATE ON THE FRAGILE-BASIS OF PUBLIC-OPINION. Society attempts to remedy all of its social-problems by examining the OPINIONS of either the people who are in trouble or causing the trouble!* We need real-answers—*answers that come not from people with problems—but from A SOURCE not connected to the people with problems, or the problems themselves.*

The Lord has revealed to me *FIVE-different-sources of information which affect people's personal decisions*: *FIVE*-different-views of each of us from *FIVE*-different-perspectives—none agreeing with any of the others!

FIRST is our own view of ourselves. Everyone views him or herself with a particular-slant! But how reliable is our own opinion of ourself? *Did OUR VIEW of ourself change as we grew up?* Has experience altered how we evaluate ourself *NOW? OUR opinion of ourself changing with time; at which time is it accurate?* Moreover, man's opinion of himself is always biased. Proverbs 16:2: "*All the ways of a man are clean IN HIS OWN EYES; but the Lord weighs the spirit.*" "*Man LOOKS upon the outward appearance, but the Lord looks on the heart.*" (1 Samuel 16:7) We develop *A DISTORTED-OPINION* of ourself by focusing on deceptive-forces; both without and within!

The *SECOND*-view: *The opinions of others about us.* Peer-pressure affects every person—not just our youth. *Keeping-up-with-the-Joneses is one compulsive-force in modern-society!* Concern over what others think of us is a major-defect of our modern-world. *Most people are compelled either to impress, or to be impressed by, their neighbors. Others' opinions of us affect the way we see ourselves!* But, there are as many different-opinions of us as there are other people! Which of those different-opinions about us is correct? We need a more-reliable-source of information about ourselves. Is it the next?

THIRD-view: Our opinion of their opinion about us. *What we think people think about us OFTEN impacts us more than what they ACTUALLY think about us! I have more than once been forced to ALTER my opinion about other people's opinions about me—because I eventually obtained the correct-information about some matter that I had earlier misunderstood.* No wonder this world is so confused! *Many-people's-decisions are based on faulty-information obtained from faulty-sources!* Moreover,...

The FOURTH-SOURCE of information about us is the most-confusing! Everybody who believes God exists has their *OWN*-opinion about *HIS*-opinion about them: And there are as many different-*OPINIONS* of God's-opinion as there are people who have opinions. *There are many different-religions on the earth; each having a different-view of the nature of God and His dealings with people!* And their-view of their-god's-nature impacts their-view of themselves! Moreover, *each religion contradicting one or more of the others, which religion is the correct-one?*

View-*FIVE*: *the way the One-True-God truly sees us. Scripture helps us to RID ourselves of all that INVALID-information about ourselves that has accumulated over time.* Romans 12:2: "*Be not conformed to the world: But be transformed BY the renewing of YOUR MIND."* Mind-renewal demands information diametrically-opposed to current-world and religious-programming. *One cannot keep THINKING, SAYING and DOING the SAME THINGS and expect different-results!* Now, *God's true-view of us is found ONLY in the Bible.* You will not regret studying Scripture. That is how we get saved and delivered from all that false-stuff the world and religion throw at us.

To answer the title-page-question: "Who determines my identity, my dignity, my destiny?" Since the Creator and Redeemer has already done *HIS PART* by planning My redemption, *AND JESUS CHRIST* has already done *HIS PART* by purchasing My redemption on that cross, *AND BOTH* Scripture and human-witnesses have done *THEIR PART* in getting the redemption-message to Me, *AND SATAN* has been stripped of any authority to keep me bound from redemption and blinded to redemption, then the *ONLY ENTITY* left in that determining-process is Me! Redemption *NOW* being accessible to me, then I am the entity that determines my identity, my dignity, my destiny! Therefore, I cannot blame anybody else if I fail to receive my-redemption, or walk in its benefits.

This book is designed to help you *LOCATE* yourself, and then *RELOCATE* yourself, if you do not like where you *FIND* yourself at present! God's Word and the Holy Spirit will help you unidentify with Adam; then identify with Christ—then reveal to you your *RICH*-inheritance in Christ—designed for both this life and the next.

This volume is not meant to be leisure-reading. It is a keepsake for those who desire to live a victorious-life in Christ. *So you will need to read it again and again to BUILD that revelation into you. Nobody can get all they need for victory from even a good book by reading it just one time! As an added-attraction, I positioned the extra-Scripture-references within the text.* I figure readers will more likely look up those *EXTRA*-Scripture-passages if they are listed in the text; not at the end of the chapter or book. It keeps all necessary information right before the readers: They are less likely to *LOSE THEIR PLACE OR ATTENTION* with that order. It is the best system of presentation I have found. And now,...

I must make one additional-observation before I go: The climate-change-argument is that, man's overuse of *SUVS*, and methane-gas from cattle, are the producers of the weird-weather-patterns in this world today. *Man and cows may have some impact upon the weather, but are they THE CAUSE of those earthquakes and volcano-eruptions happening IN INCREASING-NUMBERS around the globe? Scientists are also reporting great-increase in solar-activity—in both number and intensity. And extra-solar-activity ALWAYS affects weather-patterns—and to a much-greater-degree than do SUVS and COWS. Also, the Bible PROPHESIES that in the-last-days-of-this-age THERE WILL BE A GREAT-INCREASE OF THOSE VERY ACTIVITIES.* (Matthew 24:6-8) And, we see them on the news every day. *We are living in those days!*

The revelation-knowledge in this volume will *EQUIP* today's-church to gain *TOTAL-VICTORY* over the world, the flesh and Satan in *BIBLICAL-PROPORTIONS*, before Christ returns. To do so, we have to personally-identify with Christ in His death, burial and resurrection. Then diligently-study God's-Inspired-Word to learn *WHO we are, WHAT we possess,* and *WHAT we may accomplish in Christ during this-lifetime and the next. So, latch onto the revelation in this book, and RUN with it!* (Habakkuk 2:2) Only your Creator and Redeemer *AND YOU* should determine your identity, your dignity, your destiny!

www.ingramcontent.com/pod-product-compliance
Lightning Source LLC
LaVergne TN
LVHW041942070526
838199LV00051BA/2876